Faith Restored

The Resurgence of Notre Dame Football

John Heisler

TRIUMPH
B O O K S

This book is available in quantity at special discounts for your group or organization. For further information, contact:

Triumph Books LLC
814 North Franklin
Chicago, Illinois 60610
(312) 337-0747
www.triumphbooks.com

Printed in U.S.A.
ISBN: 978-1-60078-861-1
Design by Patricia Frey
Editorial production by Alex Lubertozzi
Photos courtesy of Michael and Susan Bennett unless otherwise indicated

Contents

Foreword

The things that were important from day one for our University of Notre Dame football program were still important in year three. When you look at it as far as breaking through, it wasn't one thing that stood out. It was just consistently asking our players to do certain things every single day and knowing they would have success. So it was just a matter of time.

I never had a particular point in time that I thought it would occur; it was just one of those things that comes together—attention to detail, getting players to buy into what we're doing in the weight room, what we're doing conditioning-wise. Really the last element to come together was how we played the game on Saturday because, in year one and year two, our players by and large did exactly what we wanted them to do. We just didn't play the game the right way on Saturday.

We went to work this year on things that cost us games. We didn't have to worry about guys buying in. We didn't have to spend time on who is going to play what position. We didn't have to spend time on rebuilding the defense. We had already addressed all that. All of those things came together, and we played the game the right way.

Winning at the end of the day is the best feature. It allows all of those leaps of faith to be solidified—telling a guy if you do it this way, we'll be successful. We told them what would happen if they did X, Y, and Z. Now what we'll do is construct teams every year based upon the personalities, not based upon how they train, how they take care of themselves in the off-season, their commitment level. We don't have to do that anymore.

I think the 2012 season could be summed up in our need to find ourselves on offense and, while we were doing that, to rely heavily on the defense, and they came through for us. The defense came through for us while we were trying to sort out the quarterback position. If we were not a strong unit defensively, we wouldn't have had the season we ended up having.

Clearly, we went in knowing there were going to be some growing pains offensively. But we made some decisions to move players to defense. KeiVarae Russell, who was a better dynamic offensive player, went to defense. Matthias Farley went to defense. We made those decisions knowing that we had to shore ourselves up defensively, and we did. And they bought us some time to get the offense to come around.

We knew we had Manti Te'o and Louis Nix to clog up the middle. I think it started with the cornerback and safety positions—kind of an uncertain area after we lost Robert Blanton and Harrison Smith to graduation. Those were two big pieces that we really weren't sure about until we played the games. Then we saw that Bennett Jackson was inexperienced at the position, but he, KeiVarae Russell, and Matthias Farley coming in for Jamoris Slaughter—they all played key roles for us.

We felt there was one guy whom we couldn't lose in 2012, and it was Jamoris Slaughter, and sure enough, we lost Jamoris in the Michigan State game. So all bets were off until we saw how these other young kids played. But once we saw them come in and really play with a lot of confidence, we felt that we were going to be okay defensively.

I wouldn't trade the opportunity to play in the Bowl Championship Series title game and what it taught our kids—how we were able to benefit from that game as a program will pay dividends for the 2013 team and beyond.

Notre Dame certainly put itself as a football program back in that limelight that it had not been in for some years. So there were many, many positives. Our players proved they could be No. 1 on the field and in graduation rates, as well.

Our football team decided it on the field. They won all their games and they were deserving of the opportunity to play for a national championship. So we'll take that any day. This is the story of that 2012 season.

—Brian Kelly
University of Notre Dame head football coach

Introduction

A New Start

In the Beginning

Brian Kelly walked to the podium in the Guglielmino Athletics Complex after being introduced by athletics director Jack Swarbrick—and, with that, the era of the latest head football coach at the University of Notre Dame officially began.

Since Lou Holtz left the Irish coaching job after the 1996 season with 100 victories in his back pocket, Notre Dame had seen more than its share of football ups and downs. Over the next 13 years, the Irish would not manage more than two consecutive winning seasons.

Bob Davie (1997–2001) took Notre Dame to its first Bowl Championship Series game in 2000 and two years earlier led the Irish to the Gator Bowl, but two of his last three years featured five-win campaigns. Tyrone Willingham (2002–2004) won eight straight games to begin his first season and saw his Irish make the cover of *Sports Illustrated*—but his final two teams finished a combined 11–13. Charlie Weis (2005–2009) led his first two teams to BCS games and 19 combined wins—but his next team ended up 3–9, and his final three years equated to a combined 16–21 mark.

What would it take for Notre Dame to regain a spot among the college football elite? Would Kelly be the guy to coach and recruit and do all the others things required on and off the field to make it work? If nothing else, Kelly was no rookie. Nineteen previous seasons as a head coach included two NCAA Division II national championships, five seasons that produced bowl invitations at Central Michigan and Cincinnati—and BCS appearances by his last two teams at Cincinnati, the 2009 version after a perfect 12–0 regular season.

A name like Kelly and a background in politics certainly couldn't hurt. Notre Dame's new head coach glibly waded through the laundry list of questions—with his parents, wife Paqui, and their three children, plus a handful of other family members watching from a middle row of the auditorium. Later that night, the Kelly delegation joined members of the Notre Dame athletics staff at dinner at the Carriage House west of South Bend. All those present had hopes that this latest marriage between the Irish football program and its new boss would flourish.

Kelly came to Notre Dame with a reputation for running the wide-open spread offense that characterized his Cincinnati teams, in particular the 2009 squad that led the nation in passing efficiency and averaged nearly 40 points per game. Three years later, in 2012, Kelly would again preside over a 12–0 regular season, this time in South Bend. But this time he didn't do it with outsized scoring efforts—instead, the 2012 Irish banked their dozen wins by leaning on a fierce defensive unit, led by all-star linebacker Manti Te'o, as well as improved physical play on both sides of the line of scrimmage. Defense became the Notre Dame hallmark, allowing an offense to steadily grow side by side with a first-year starter at quarterback.

This is the story of how Kelly and his Notre Dame football program evolved and laid the bricks to go from consecutive 8–5 campaigns in 2010 and 2011 to a perfect regular season and Bowl Championship Series title game appearance in 2012. We'll take you month by month and, often, day by day as the 2012 season unfolded and the Irish found themselves back in the national championship conversation once again.

Chapter 1

The Off-season

Tuesday, January 10

Notre Dame athletics director Jack Swarbrick announced that the University has exercised an option in football coach Brian Kelly's contract and extended it for two years, now through the 2016 season. That came eight days after contract renewals were announced for returning Irish assistant coaches.

Wednesday, January 11

Notre Dame ranks 23rd in the early 2012 football preview poll by ESPN.com's Mark Schlabach. The 2012 Irish schedule features more than its share of expected top-flight opponents—and here's where they ranked in three published 2012 preseason polls:

Opponent	ESPN.com	CBSSports.com	Yahoo! Sports
USC	No. 2	No. 2	No. 2
Oklahoma	No. 5	No. 7	No. 5

Michigan State	No. 9	No. 18	No. 13
Michigan	No. 11	No. 10	No. 8
Stanford	No. 17	NR	No. 20

The Irish in 2012 face Michigan (September 22) and Stanford (October 13) at Notre Dame Stadium—while going on the road to meet Michigan State (September 15), Oklahoma (October 27), and USC (November 24).

All the various bloggers for ESPN.com took an early look at the major football conferences for 2012—and here's where they rated teams Notre Dame faces in 2012:

- Michigan State: No. 1 in Big Ten
- Michigan: No. 2 in Big Ten
- Purdue: No. 8 in Big Ten
- Wake Forest: No. 7 in ACC
- Boston College: No. 9 in ACC
- Miami: No. 10 in ACC
- Pittsburgh: No. 6 in Big East
- USC: No. 1 in Pac-12
- Stanford: No. 4 in Pac-12
- Oklahoma: No. 1 in Big 12

Yet another (very) early preseason top 25 poll for 2012 college football came from Andy Staples at SI.com—and it lists Notre Dame 22nd. Irish opponents in 2012 on that same list include USC (second), Michigan State (sixth), Oklahoma (eighth), Michigan (11th), and Stanford (20th).

Friday, January 20

Irish tight end Tyler Eifert spent the weekend in New Haven, Connecticut, for the Walter Camp awards dinner, honoring 2011 Camp All-America selections.

Saturday, January 21

With assistant coaches Tim Hinton and Ed Warinner departing to join Urban Meyer's new staff at Ohio State, Brian Kelly filled one of those vacancies by hiring veteran assistant Bob Elliott, who most recently has coached the secondary at Iowa State the last two seasons. Elliott has been in the business 33 years, working with defensive backs in 22 of those seasons. He's been a defensive coordinator for 11 combined seasons at San Diego State, Kansas State, Iowa, and Ball State—and he also has coached at Kent State and North Carolina. Elliott comes from a football family—he played at Iowa, where his father, Bump, was athletics director. And chemistry with the current Irish coaches comes ready-made: during Elliott's stint at Iowa, he coached current Irish assistant Kerry Cooks (a Hawkeyes captain in 1997) and also worked with current Irish assistant Bob Diaco when Diaco both played (1991–1995) and coached (graduate assistant in 1996–1997) at Iowa. Elliott's time at Iowa mirrored that of current Irish football strength and conditioning director Paul Longo.

Wednesday, January 25

Brian Kelly took care of the second staff opening by adding veteran Harry Hiestand as offensive line coach and run-game coordinator. With 29 years of experience behind him, Hiestand has spent the last 15 years either in the NFL or at Big Ten or Southeastern Conference schools—including stints with the Chicago Bears and at Tennessee and Illinois.

Hiestand most recently has been at the University of Tennessee for two seasons and also has coached at Missouri, Cincinnati, Toledo, USC (graduate assistant), and Penn. He played at both Springfield (Massachusetts) College and East Stroudsburg. Hiestand and Elliott combined represent a solid influx of experience for the Irish staff.

As it relates to the challenges of different jobs, every one poses a new challenge, that Coach Kelly, in short order, figures out and assimilates. [Former Iowa] Coach [Hayden] Fry used to say, "Scratch where it itches." Going from Grand Valley to Central Michigan and Division I-A recruiting, he dove into that. Then moving from Mount Pleasant, Michigan, to a spectacular city in Cincinnati, he assimilated into that culture. Then Notre Dame and Notre Dame's distinctions fit him and his world nicely. So I would say it's been about the normal growth he's had at every institution where he's worked.

—Assistant head coach and defensive coordinator Bob Diaco

Wednesday, February 1

Brian Kelly and his staff put the finishing touches on their third recruiting class by signing 17 high school seniors to national letters of intent, while also adding one transfer student to the Irish roster. Four of those 18 players—transfer running back Amir Carlisle (from USC), early-enrollee freshmen defensive lineman Sheldon Day, quarterback Gunner Kiel, and defensive back Tee Shepard—began taking classes at Notre Dame in January. They will participate in Notre Dame's spring football practices that begin March 21. The other 14 players will arrive on campus by June 18 for the start of summer school. Among the 17 players who will be freshmen for the Irish this fall are four who were selected for the U.S. Army All-American Bowl in San Antonio: defensive lineman Jarron Jones, Kiel, running back KeiVarae Russell, and defensive back Elijah Shumate.

"Last year was about the power position. This year was about the skill level, especially the defensive backfield and the wide receiver positions. We feel like we addressed those needs," said Kelly.

Signing day is generally a giddy scene, yet there's no way to know how quickly or when any of the individual players will play a part. By the end of the 2012 campaign, six of these newcomers will play enough of a role to win monograms—Romeo Okwara, Russell (he ended up playing at cornerback after originally being listed as a running back), Shumate, Day, receiver Chris Brown, and defensive back Nicky Baratti.

Tuesday, February 21

The *Athlon* 2012 college football early top 25 has Notre Dame 18th— with Irish opponents USC second, Oklahoma fifth, Michigan seventh, and Michigan State 14th. Here's what the preview says about the Irish: "Is 2012 the year the Irish get back into a BCS bowl? Although Notre Dame has some key pieces returning, this team is probably ticketed for a spot in the lower half of the top 25 next year. Settling on a quarterback is priority No. 1 for coach Brian Kelly this spring. True freshman Gunner Kiel is already enrolled and will have a good shot to beat out Tommy Rees, Andrew Hendrix, and Everett Golson in preseason practices. With uncertainty at quarterback, expect running back Cierre Wood and a solid offensive line to carry the team early on. The defense will have a revamped secondary, but the line—led by Aaron Lynch, Louis Nix, and Stephon Tuitt—could be one of the best in college football."

Saturday, March 3

Irish defensive back Chris Salvi fought tonight for the 188-pound title in the Bengal Bouts (he won in a three-round split decision), Notre Dame's club boxing tournament that benefits the missions of Bangladesh. And his younger brother, Will, also advanced to the finals, though another commitment kept him from competing. That's the sort of toughness any football coach can appreciate.

From a player's point of view, coach [Kelly] this past off-season and in the winter took time out of his schedule to just meet with his us—not to talk about Xs and Os. He just talked to us as individuals, about school and how we're doing, how we're doing socially. It was an opportunity for us to get to know him better and an opportunity for him to get to know us. That has definitely shown itself on the field and in the bond that we have with him, and the trust that we have in him, not only in the things he does, but how he leads this team. Every player trusts him, not only for the success that we've had as a team, but what he's done for us off the field."

—*Linebacker Manti Te'o*

Chapter 2

Spring Drills

Tuesday, March 20

The day before the Irish began spring drills, coach Brian Kelly offered his thoughts on the formal start of his third year on the field with the Irish. Kelly confirms six fifth-year applications that have been approved by the Faculty Board on Athletics—meaning that on an official basis veterans Mike Golic Jr., Jamoris Slaughter, Kapron Lewis-Moore, Braxston Cave, John Goodman, and Dan McCarthy will play in 2012.

Not surprisingly, the first question out of the box—and it's one Kelly will address regularly for the next five months—involves the quarterback situation, with incumbent Tommy Rees, Andrew Hendrix, Everett Golson (he didn't play at all as a freshman in 2011), and early-enrolled rookie Gunner Kiel all on the roster. The Irish coaches will attempt to give all four a chance to compete, though as Kelly noted, "If we started the spring with page 50 of the playbook, Tommy would be ahead of everybody."

Here's more from Kelly from when he met the media:

- "It starts and ends with the quarterback position. It's important they are going to get an equal opportunity to compete for the position, so they all have to start with a very similar knowledge base. So we've kind of taken a step back. We want the ball to come out of the quarterback's hands in a timely fashion and for good decisions to be made. We threw way too many interceptions last year, and it certainly affected our win-loss record."
- The Irish held their own combine and created measurements and timings in a variety of pro-day areas for their players (10- and 20- and 40-yard dash times, broad jump, vertical jump, cone drills, etc.).
- "In year three it's a comfortable feeling because I'm confident I know my football team very well going in."
- Sophomore-to-be Troy Niklas moves from outside linebacker to tight end.
- Sophomore-to-be receiver DaVaris Daniels produced the best testing numbers of all the Irish skill position players.
- Look for Theo Riddick and John Goodman to start as the punt returners.

The offense at that point was still a legitimate four-horse race at quarterback, which is not exactly what you want. Starting the spring was about how we practiced, how we developed a mentality on offense, and how we're never going to turn the ball over. With the quarterback scenario, you're trying to give more kids reps and understanding that long-term we've got to figure this out. Short-term it would be easy to go with the guy who's ahead now because we need to get reps and get better.

—*Chuck Martin*

Saturday, March 24

All four of the Irish quarterback candidates were available to the media after today's noon practice, so the analysis of the Notre Dame signal-calling derby is ongoing.

Thursday, April 5

The Notre Dame Monogram Club added 61 new members, including 20 Irish football players, to its roster tonight at Club Naimoli at Purcell Pavilion in its letter-jacket ceremony for fall sports. Deputy athletics director Bill Scholl represented the athletics department and compared the Irish athletics program to an Olympic village: "It's not for the faint of heart. If you want to compete at the highest level, this is the place to be." Former Notre Dame football All-American Allen Pinkett served as the guest speaker, saying, "No one can represent the University the way you do." Senior football player Brandon Newman represented the monogram winners, saying, "All of my life I wanted to be part of something special. When I was a junior in high school, I received a call from the Notre Dame football program. I knew nothing about Notre Dame. I had no idea how that phone call would change my life." Notre Dame president Reverend John I. Jenkins, C.S.C., offered the benediction and remarks: "Some day your participation in athletics is going to come to an end. Friendship, courage, dedication, sacrifice, a willingness to work—that's what you'll take from your experiences as a student-athlete. In the end, those qualities are the true victories."

Friday, April 13

Brian Kelly traveled to Chicago tonight and spent a half-hour addressing the 650 attendees at the Notre Dame Club of Chicago's 54th Rockne Awards Banquet—with Kelly making some opening remarks and then participating in a lengthy Q-and-A session with WNDU-TV sports director Jeff Jeffers.

Here are some of Kelly's offerings:

- On the quarterback situation: "We must eliminate turnovers. It's exciting to work and teach these guys as we go through that process."

- On Notre Dame's starting tight end: "We think we've got one of the finest offensive talents in the country in Tyler Eifert. We're going to make it difficult on teams—we're going move him all over the place, like we did with Michael Floyd last year."
- On what he likes about the spring so far: "I like the development of our offensive and defensive lines. They continue to be the strength of our football team."
- On the Notre Dame job in general: "I wanted this challenge—it's about bridging to the past by achieving success in the present. If you own any stock in Notre Dame football, you're going to start seeing some dividends."
- On the 2012 schedule: "You've got to start with a win, you've got to win your home games, and you've got to win your rivalry games. If you can do that, you're in pretty good shape."

Though Kelly assessed the individual talents of each of the four quarterback candidates, he offered no hints as to which one might have staked any sort of claim to the No. 1 slot.

Friday, April 20

There's plenty of interest in Irish football this weekend. The ESPN college football bus is on campus today to do interviews with Brian Kelly and Irish players. Kelly also meets with the announcing crew in advance of the NBC Sports Network live telecast of the Blue-Gold game on Saturday.

Former Irish players Sergio Brown and Golden Tate will serve as honorary captains for the flag football game featuring former Irish players at 11:00 AM Saturday at Notre Dame Stadium.

Almost 200 former Irish players and their families attend the dinner tonight at Purcell Pavilion, sponsored by the Notre Dame Monogram Club. The current Notre Dame team also takes part in that event.

Notre Dame vice president and athletics director Jack Swarbrick takes note of the celebration of 125 years of Notre Dame football in 2012, saying, "That's a legacy and culture worth celebrating." He detailed the origin of Notre Dame football in 1887 when the Irish played their first game against Michigan. "So, collectively, the culture of Notre Dame football has been built for 125 years—and, more so than anything else, I think we have the culture right to build for the next 125 years."

Kelly, addressing the former players, said, "This isn't meet the team night. This is our opportunity to thank you for what you've done for Notre Dame football. We continue to build our program on a day-to-day basis. Our players understand what it takes to maintain the standards you've set. We're excited about the schedule—our players have embraced it."

Kelly introduced current players Zeke Motta and John Goodman, who offered brief remarks. Motta suggested that the former players in attendance "set the bar on and off the field." Goodman noted that the current squad is modeling itself as the A Team—emphasizing accountability, achievement, and appreciation.

Former Irish star and two-time Super Bowl champion Justin Tuck offered some moving remarks (and received a standing ovation when he finished speaking) about the meaning of being at Notre Dame: "When they ask what Notre Dame means to you, you can get five different answers and they're all right."

Tuck recalled hearing former Irish defensive lineman Mike Golic (who happened to be sitting a table away) a few years back talking about finishing up at Notre Dame, packing his car, driving past the main circle, seeing the Dome in the rear-view mirror, and realizing he was no longer a student-athlete at Notre Dame. Said Tuck, "And you pulled over and cried?" Offered Golic, "No, I cried and just kept driving."

Tuck talked about how he decided to come to Notre Dame, despite having offers from all the Southeastern Conference schools and despite visiting the Notre Dame campus with a significant amount of snow on the ground. Said Tuck, "I get goose bumps when I fly over the stadium, when I walk by the Dome, when I watch you guys play on NBC. It took me four years to realize it. I hope it doesn't take you that long. I'll be rooting for you. I'll fight for you. Believe me, I bleed blue and gold."

The Meet the Irish brunch Saturday morning featuring Kelly and the Irish squad has been sold out for weeks. A crowd of 1,000 is expected, with remarks from the Notre Dame head coach and a player autograph session following the brunch.

Saturday, April 21

The Irish finished their spring drills in front of more than 31,000 fans at Notre Dame Stadium in the annual Blue-Gold contest. Most of the fans came to see what the Irish quarterback derby might display—and they watched Everett Golson complete 11 of 15 passes for 120 yards and a pair of scores. Running back George Atkinson III contributed 124 rushing yards on 15 attempts, while Theo Riddick snared eight receptions for 63 yards. Linebacker Kendall Moore led with eight tackles, while corner Lo Wood had seven and Anthony Rabasa six.

With a roster not complete enough to field two full teams, the game featured point-scoring opportunities for both the offense and defense, and the defensive unit ended up winning 42–31. Chris Salvi, Matthias Farley, and Ishaq Williams all had interceptions.

Former Irish football standout Justin Tuck, who helped the New York Giants win the Super Bowl in February, was honored on the field before the game.

Vice president and athletics director Jack Swarbrick and coach Brian Kelly took part in a "conversation" tonight on the concourse of the Joyce Center, fielding a variety of questions submitted by those in attendance at the Notre Dame Monogram Club Annual Dinner. Here are some of their offerings:

BK "The building blocks of any successful program are consistency and stability. You want to know what to expect on a day-to-day basis. We've got some work to do."

JS On the ongoing BCS talks and conference realignment: "The goal and priority is to remain independent [in football]. What the postseason becomes is the lynchpin. There's still one chapter to come as far as conference realignment, and that will come after these BCS discussions. These are an important three and a half days [of meetings] this next week in Florida. [The result] will have a significant impact on us one way or another."

BK On recruiting: "We talk about the distinctions [at Notre Dame]. You're shopping down a different aisle. We talk about faith, about community, about living in the residence halls. We lay our cards on the table. We want to make sure you don't come here under false pretenses."

JS On potential compensation for student-athletes: "One question is about whether or not we adequately reflect the cost of attendance. I'm part of an NCAA committee that's looking at that. Does a student-athlete have the same means necessary to have the same experience as anyone else on campus? A number of our student-athletes are here in summer school and can't have a full-time summer job. So what we're talking about is different than compensating student-athletes. If you attend Notre Dame and also receive a Pell Grant, that's the equivalent of about $70,000—that's a fair deal."

BK On early enrollees: "It's a great opportunity if they feel as a family that we can provide an early entrance to college life. At Notre Dame you're going to be locked down and ready to go from an academic standpoint."

Chapter 3

Summer in South Bend

Tuesday, May 29

Irish linebacker Manti Te'o graces the cover of the national edition of the *Athlon* 2012 college football preview magazine, including these other Irish mentions:

- Te'o and Tyler Eifert both are projected as first-team All-Americans.
- The list of NFL Draft–eligible prospects has Te'o ninth and Eifert 31st.
- *Athlon* rates Notre Dame's quarterback battle in the fall as the second best in the country (behind Oregon's).
- It lists the jeweled shillelagh that Notre Dame and USC battle for as the second best rivalry trophy (behind the Floyd of Rosedale pig that goes to the Iowa-Minnesota winner).
- The list of top 12 nonconference games has Notre Dame–Oklahoma on October 27 rated second, Notre Dame–Michigan on September 22 third, Notre Dame–USC on November 24 seventh, Notre Dame–Miami on October 6 10th and Notre Dame–Navy from Dublin on September 1 12th.
- Notre Dame's 2012 recruiting class is rated 20th.

- Among the top 100 incoming freshmen, Gunner Kiel is 20th overall.
- In recruiting position rankings, Notre Dame is fourth for quarterbacks, 10th for defensive tackles, eighth for defensive backs.
- The Irish are rated 33rd for 2012, with upcoming Notre Dame opponents USC second, Oklahoma fourth, Michigan seventh, Michigan State 12th, and Stanford 21st.
- In player ratings, Cierre Wood is 18th among running backs, Eifert first among tight ends, Te'o first among inside linebackers.

This summer, it wasn't a moment, but it was a sign that this team was different. It wasn't a sign that said, man, we're going to make it to the national championship. It was just a sign that said, hey, this team is different, this team is willing to sacrifice a lot. We had a pretty hard conditioning workout in the summer, and our coaches gave us the option of doing that day's lift in the weight room. They said, "It's optional. You can do it if you want. I understand that a lot of you are going to be tired and exhausted after this workout." And we were, but every single one of our players slowly worked their way into the weight room and did their lift, and nobody asked anybody, nobody forced anyone, but the leaders went, and the rest followed. It was just one of those moments where we said, okay, we have a chance here. We constantly worked every day and focused on the day's tasks and were making sure that by the end of the day we were better than the start.

—Manti Te'o

Friday, June 1

Here's what *Phil Steele's 2012 College Football Preview* says about Notre Dame:

- Both TE Tyler Eifert and LB Manti Te'o are listed as preseason first-team All-Americans.

- In position rankings, Tommy Rees is the No. 55 quarterback, Cierre Wood the No. 15 running back, Theo Roddick No. 48 at running back, TJ Jones No. 45 among receivers, Eifert No. 1 at tight end, Braxston Cave No. 8 at center, Chris Watt No. 23 at guard, Zack Martin No. 18 at offensive tackle, Kapron Lewis-Moore No. 2 at defensive end, Louis Nix No. 46 at defensive tackle, Te'o No. 1 at inside linebacker, Prince Shembo No. 48 at outside linebacker, Bennett Jackson No. 34 at cornerback, Jamoris Slaughter No. 15 at strong safety, Zeke Motta No. 36 at free safety.
- In unit rankings, the Irish were No. 37 at quarterback, No. 17 at running back, No. 16 at receiver, No. 11 at offensive line, No. 22 at defensive line, No. 8 at linebacker, No. 28 on special teams.
- The Irish are No. 21 in preseason rankings.
- Among incoming freshmen, Gunner Kiel is the No. 1 quarterback, KeiVarae Russell No. 18 at running back, Will Mahone No. 23 at running back, Davonte Neal No. 8 at receiver, Justin Ferguson No. 43 at receiver, Ronnie Stanley No. 20 at offensive line, Mark Harrell No. 61 at offensive line, Jarron Jones No. 20 on defensive line, Sheldon Day No. 23 on defensive line, Elijah Shumate No. 15 at defensive back, C.J. Prosise No. 56 at defensive back. The Irish freshman class is rated No. 9 overall.
- Phil Steele says Notre Dame has the toughest overall schedule for 2012—with the Irish slate ranked fourth in terms of opponent win-loss percentage (.634) based on 2011 results.

The 2012 *USA Today* college football preview magazine has Wood on the cover of its national edition. Eifert and Te'o both are listed as preseason first-team All-Americans (as they have been on every preseason list to date). Notre Dame is rated 19th on a preseason basis.

Tuesday, June 12

The Kelly Cares Foundation, the charity founded by Brian Kelly and his wife, Paqui, cohosted the third edition of Football 101 tonight. Football 101 gives women at least 21 years old a tutorial session on football basics, an opportunity to meet the Notre Dame football coaching staff, learn Fighting Irish football trivia, and enjoy a taste of upscale area restaurants. Participants also get a behind-the-scenes look at the Guglielmino Athletics Complex and LaBar Practice Complex (football practice fields). The Fighting Irish coaching staff teaches the basics of football form and technique, including passing, catching, and kicking on the LaBar practice fields. Inside the Gug's football meeting rooms, other members of the coaching staff will teach the fundamental Xs and Os of the game, helping participants learn concepts such as how missed blocks and route-running can make the difference between a sack and a touchdown. The evening concludes with a fashion show of athletic gear and football equipment. Proceeds from Football 101 benefit breast cancer prevention, awareness, and early detection initiatives chosen by the Kelly Cares Foundation.

Monday, June 25

Fans of college football and the game of golf helped three innovative charities and met Notre Dame coaching legends Ara Parseghian and Lou Holtz plus current Irish football coach Brian Kelly today at the annual Irish Legends Charity Golf, Dinner, and Auction Classic at Lost Dunes Golf Club in Bridgman, Michigan, and Point O'Woods Golf and Country Club in Benton Harbor, Michigan. The dinner and auction, hosted by ESPN personality Mark May, was at Lost Dunes. Proceeds from the event supported Ara Parseghian Medical Research Foundation, Lou Holtz Charitable Foundation, and Kelly Cares Foundation.

Chapter 4

Fall Camp

Friday, August 3

The interesting thing about Brian Kelly, he's had so much success, and yet most of the people I know who have had as much success as him in life get stuck on their plan. This is my plan, and this is what's made me successful. And there are certain things within our program from all the way back to 2000 at Grand Valley [State] that haven't changed. Those are some things Brian Kelly has believed in, big picture, for a long time, and it's served him well.

But the piece for him that's been a separator is his willingness to adapt. His style of football team isn't cookie cutter—this is how I want it, this is how I want to win it, and we're going to be a pro-I, smashmouth offense. Even at Grand Valley, over 13 years, he changed his style of play. He changed from pro to spread, or we changed for this style of defense to this style of defense. He always looks at his personnel and gets the most out of his resources.

A lot of it has to do with his willingness to say, how is Notre Dame going to win? And I think that was a three-year process. He won 12 games in Cincinnati in '09. He won 12 games in 2012, and they didn't look like the same style. You don't come in and know exactly what the campus is like, but you look at it and decide these are the kids who are going to flourish at Notre Dame. So I think going into year three, he said, this is how Notre Dame's going to have the success that I'm going to demand. I'm not necessarily going to say that we did it this way at Grand Valley or Central Michigan or Cincinnati. Most people who have had his successes don't ever bend on anything.

—Chuck Martin

As you might guess, when Brian Kelly held his opening press conference today in advance of the start of fall camp, many of the questions revolved around the quarterback situation. Here's what Kelly offered:

- "We have to have a quarterback we can trust who's going to take great care of the football and get us in the right place. As we move forward here, it's developing that trust with our quarterbacks and not accepting anything less than that level of trust of taking care of the football. That was the emphasis in the spring, and that will continue to be the emphasis. But the starting quarterback against Navy is a guy we believe carries those traits with him, and we can trust that he's going to make good decisions."
- "I think early on we've got to be able to see three quarterbacks. As we move closer to finding if there is a separation, then we'll start to separate the reps. But we don't go into practice once saying, okay, he's getting 80 percent, he's getting 20, or he's getting 70/30. We're not at that point. It's going to take some time for us to figure that out in terms of who is going to get those reps. But ultimately we want to be able to give the quarterback for Navy a lot of reps leading into the game. Where we start is: we've got to be able to evaluate them based upon what they did this summer, then start to close in on what that pecking order is. So I don't know the exact date, but we'll know it when we see it."

- "It's going to take some practices for us to even get the reps to separate. So, for me to have a date in mind, ideally we'd like to in a week's time say, 'All right, here's your quarterback.' That's what everybody would want to do because then you get the continuity with your offense. We just have to take this one practice at a time before we get into those specifics."

- "I think everything's on the table. I don't know if we've taken anything off the table relative to the quarterback position. Ideally, I'm like everybody else in this room. I'd like to have one quarterback and have him be the guy, but we won't know until we get out there and put the pads on, get live action, and see how these guys react to those scenarios and situations."

- "If we get the guy, and he starts against Navy and he doesn't play very well, I don't want him to start next week, nor do you. But I would like, like everybody else, to prepare somebody and have a great game against Navy and then make it a difficult decision what you do in Week 2."

- "I don't want to make this more than it is. I have not decided. The question was asked, 'Do you have an idea?' I've got an idea, but an idea is all I have. It's not like it's this guy and we are set for it, or I would be less than honest in answering the question relative to reps. I've got an idea, but we have to see how this plays out. We have to rep these guys, we have to give them a lot of work, a lot of situations. We'll be doing a lot more 11-on-11, where we have to put our players, in particular the quarterback, in as many situations that put 11 players out on the field at one time. Half-line, seven-on-seven, inside drill—all great drills—don't get the quarterback to the level that we need to. So a lot more 11-on-11 reps for this football team to help us answer that question."

Sunday, August 12

There's nothing on the practice field today, but the players lift weights and have a special team meeting and offensive and defensive walk-throughs.

Monday, August 13

Today's afternoon practice is Professor Appreciation Day, as Notre Dame faculty and their families are invited to watch the Irish work out, followed by a photo session.

Thursday, August 16

After morning position meetings, it's media day for the Fighting Irish players and coaches, with interview sessions in the Notre Dame Stadium press box, followed by a team photo in the stands, and then video head shots in the locker room.

Saturday, August 18

The players have the day off, with University orientation activities going on in advance of the start of classes on Tuesday.

Tuesday, August 21

Brian Kelly today indicated that both Everett Golson and Andrew Hendrix continue to share reps during football practice, and no decision has been made on a quarterback starter for the Navy game (with Tommy Rees not an option for the opener). Said Kelly, "The quarterbacks are still developing. They both continue to get better every day." Kelly also noted that expected cornerback starter Lo Wood suffered a ruptured Achilles tendon Monday night in practice, will have surgery Wednesday, and miss the entire 2012 season. He is expected back for 2013 spring drills. The Irish have five other cornerbacks on the roster, led by Bennett Jackson. Said Kelly, "Besides Bennett, there are four other guys who we know can play the position, and now they are on stage. They all know they are right there."

Thursday, August 23

Brian Kelly officially announced after practice today that Everett Golson will be the starting Notre Dame quarterback in the September 1 opener in Dublin against Navy.

In August we make the decision to go with the young guy we knew legitimately needed time in the cooker. We knew long-term this was going to be the best for our football program moving forward. That's why coach made the decision to go with the kid who won the job at camp and won it based on having the most ability. But no one envisioned in fall camp Tommy [Rees] was going to help us win four games. It became a Disney movie, but if Disney wrote it, no one would believe it could really happen.

—*Chuck Martin*

Saturday, August 25

As heavy workouts wind down, the Irish squad heads to Notre Dame Stadium to go through its pregame warm-up routine and a "bench control" practice. Sunday is a day off for the squad.

The Notre Dame football coaches may be worried about what can possibly go wrong when you take your team across an ocean to play a football game in unfamiliar territory. Nonetheless, the Fighting Irish trip to Ireland to open the season against Navy is only a week away, and there's no shortage of interesting logistical and cultural items:

- Anthony Travel, the official travel partner with the Naval Academy (and with Notre Dame) for the Notre Dame–Navy game in Dublin next week, is doing business with 120 hotels in the Dublin area and will have 90 staff members on the ground in Dublin coordinating travel and events. By the time the game weekend is over, Anthony Travel will have invested more than 50,000 man-hours in the planning and execution of the event. More than 3,500 boxes containing itineraries, tickets, and other travel materials have been sent via FedEx to those traveling to Dublin for the game. Over the course of three nights in Dublin, Anthony Travel will entertain a combined 5,000 guests at private events at the Guinness Storehouse.

- The listed capacity at Aviva Stadium is 50,000—with all seats covered by the roof. For this game, the capacity will be 48,000, since the first six rows will be tarped due to less-than-ideal sight lines.
- Here's where the 48,000 game tickets went:
  - 25,000 were sold through the Navy and Notre Dame athletics tickets offices. Notre Dame (as the visiting team) received 7,500 tickets. They were offered via a lottery to contributing alumni, with more than 14,700 requests for those 7,500 tickets.
  - 13,000 were sold in Dublin via Ticketmaster Ireland and CSL Hospitality.
  - 10,000 were offered by Anthony Travel via various travel packages.
- The Notre Dame–Navy game will be the first game that the Notre Dame football team's video crew shoots fully in HD. The biggest challenge for Tim Collins and his staff is handling power conversion issues at the team hotel and at Aviva Stadium.
- More than 100 passport applications have been processed over the last few months with the help of the Notre Dame Post Office for Fighting Irish players, coaches, and other staff members. Required photos of the incoming freshman players were taken once they reported to campus in June for the start of summer school. The biggest challenge came in locating certified birth certificates for all applicants—as well as cutting multiple checks through the athletics business office for each of the passports.

- The Fighting Irish will buy oxygen for use on the sideline in Ireland, since it cannot be taken on the team plane.
- Notre Dame athletic trainers made arrangements to drop-ship cases of Gatorade in advance of the game for use in Dublin.
- ESPN America will take the television feed from CBS and air the game in 66 countries in Europe, the Middle East, and Africa.
- American Forces Network will also carry the CBS television feed to 175 countries and U.S. Territories. The American Forces Network worldwide radio and television broadcast network serves American service men and women, Department of Defense, and other U.S. government civilians and their families stationed at bases overseas, as well as U.S. Navy ships at sea.
- There have been close to 200 media members credentialed for the game with newspapers from Japan, Germany, Austria, Italy, France, the United Kingdom, Poland, and Hungary covering the contest along with numerous media outlets from Ireland, Northern Ireland, and the United States.
- The equipment that will accompany the Notre Dame team on its flight weighs 15,000 to 20,000 pounds.
- Aviva Stadium is the home of Ireland's national rugby and soccer (football, by Irish parlance) programs, including the site of RBS 6 Nations rugby games each spring. Recent concerts at Aviva include Madonna (July 24) and Lady Gaga (September 15). The stadium opened in May 2010. It was built on the site of the famed Lansdowne Road Stadium (the oldest sports stadium in Europe) that originally opened in 1876.
- One member of the current Notre Dame football team actually attended the 1996 Notre Dame–Navy game at Croke Park. Sophomore offensive

lineman Conor Hanratty attended that game as a three-year-old with his father, former Fighting Irish All-America quarterback Terry Hanratty.

Wondering about the international interest level for the Notre Dame–Navy football game in Dublin? Beyond those who routinely cover the two teams, here are some of the other media outlets that have been credentialed:

- BPA Sport Presse, Footballtoday CS Sports, Sander Creative Network, HUDDLE (all from Germany)
- Sports Report (from Austria)
- Football American and The Blue Pennant (both from France)
- Color Sport Images, ESPN America, *The American Magazine*, Action Sports Photography, Action Plus Sports Images (all from the United Kingdom)
- NFL 24 (from Poland)
- Irish Network Japan (from Japan)
- Nemzeti Sport (from Hungary)

In terms of mainstream Irish media, the *Irish Times* (based in Dublin) has requested seven press-box seats for its writers.

Monday, August 27

Brian Kelly tonight named his four team captains for the 2012 Irish season—linebacker Manti Te'o, defensive end Kapron Lewis-Moore, tight end Tyler Eifert, and offensive tackle Zack Martin. All four players addressed the squad and offered their thoughts on being named captains.

I think that for myself and the other three captains, Kap [Kapron Lewis-Moore], Zack [Martin], and Tyler [Eifert], we all take that very seriously. For us to have the opportunity to represent our team and to represent them every Saturday, for people to recognize us as we come out of the tunnel—with that comes a lot of responsibility. I'm just very, very blessed to be able to represent this team and to be part of this team and this journey that we've taken.

—*Manti Te'o*

Tuesday, August 28

Said Irish coach Brian Kelly at his regular weekly media conference: "You are going to need your media guide as it relates to the receiving corps because they are all going to play."

Wednesday, August 29

The Fighting Irish traveling party departs for Dublin out of Michiana Regional Airport in South Bend after practice via a Delta Airbus 330 charter that seats nearly 300 people. It seems like just another road trip—but seven hours in a plane is a bit more than the players are used to.

By the time the fight departs, it already has been a long day for the Notre Dame football team. As the Fighting Irish begin to acclimate to a five-hour time difference (and a 9:00 AM Eastern kickoff) for their Saturday matchup with Navy in Dublin, coach Brian Kelly scheduled a 6:00 AM practice today. Kelly said he breathed a "sigh of relief" at 5:20 AM when all players were accounted for because, "I made it clear anyone not on time was staying in South Bend."

Today's early-morning workout was the equivalent of a normal Thursday practice, including down-and-distance and late-game situational work, according to Kelly. This afternoon, the Notre Dame players met, weight trained, left via bus for the Michiana Regional Airport a little after 5:00 PM, then took off on their Delta charter at 6:45 PM. Kelly said he hopes the players will sleep during the flight.

Kelly said this won't be the first time he has been to Ireland. He previously made a trip to the west coast of Ireland to play golf. "I really enjoyed it and I learned a lot about Ireland," he said.

In his last visit with about 20 media members before his team left for Ireland, Kelly said he feels good about his 2012 squad even though there are several spots with young and inexperienced players. Said Kelly, "It makes you confident when you feel like you can run the football and stop the run on defense."

Thursday, August 30

There was a definite green theme to Notre Dame's overnight flight to Dublin. The Fighting Irish players and most of the coaches and football staff wore bright green sweatsuits and hats. Ask for water and it comes with a lime and a miniature Irish flag. The inside of the Delta plane was festooned with green.

The flight arrived in Ireland a half-hour early but had to wait about 20 minutes because there was no gate available at the Dublin airport. There were racks of Notre Dame and Navy gear on sale the minute the Notre Dame traveling party passed through customs and entered the Aer Lingus terminal. By the time the team buses pulled out a little before 8:00 AM, the sun shone brightly and there was not a cloud in the sky.

The Fighting Irish squad had time to get organized and eat a 10:00 AM breakfast at its Ritz-Carlton Powerscourt headquarters hotel. Notre Dame is staying about a half-hour south of the Dublin city center, a short walk from the tiny village of Enniskerry in the Wicklow mountain foothills, and a few kilometers from Bray, home of Irish Olympic boxing champion Katie Taylor. The team jumped on buses at 10:45 AM to head to Aviva Stadium—with six members of the Garda providing a motorcycle escort.

Notre Dame's team normally wears black Adidas shoes for its games, but against Navy the Fighting Irish squad will wear a special orange, green, and white Adidas shoes modeled after the colors of the Irish flag.

The Fighting Irish squad practiced for about 90 minutes in shorts on the Aviva practice pitch (artificial turf) in extremely windy conditions, with a large group of mostly Irish media interviewing coach Brian Kelly and captains Kapron Lewis-Moore, Manti Te'o, Tyler Eifert, and Zack Martin after the workout ended.

Among practice visitors was a group representing the Belfast Trojans, who won the Ireland American football title this summer. The team reps brought with them the 2012 Shamrock Bowl they won and had their picture taken with the crystal cup and Kelly.

After practice, Kelly's squad headed to Taylors Three Rock Pub in Rathfarnham for a late lunch and an exhibition of Irish dancing. The team ate dinner at its hotel and retired early after two days that seemingly became one.

Friday, August 31

The Notre Dame football team headed back to Aviva Stadium for a midday walk-through in shorts. An off-and-on drizzle and cloudy skies kept the Fighting Irish off the Aviva pitch and sent them to the artificial practice turf area just outside.

Following the workout, the players jumped into three double-decker buses (with open-air tops) for a tour of the Dublin city center and other spots in the downtown area—ending at Dublin Castle where the squad held its team Mass.

Soccer, rugby, and native Irish sports hurling and Gaelic football dominate the local sports pages, but the *Irish Times* today included a four-page tabloid-style section on the Notre Dame–Navy event.

The 90-minute Friday evening "pep rally" event at the O2 proved a resounding success as a packed house of partisan and receptive Notre Dame fans watched and listened to interviews with Notre Dame president Reverend John Jenkins, C.S.C., and vice president and athletics director Jack Swarbrick, performances by the Band of the Fighting Irish, plus a variety of well-known Irish musical stars.

Chapter 5

September

Saturday, September 1

It's game day in a foreign country and the weather is just about perfect—temperature about 60 and partly sunny. There had been two public sales of tickets in Dublin—with the seats only available if you had an Irish mailing address—and they were snapped up quickly. In the days leading up to the game, there were thousands of American visitors enjoying the Dublin area, but you never saw anyone trying to unload game tickets. If you came this far, apparently you were going to the game.

The Naval Academy opted to print a smaller, European-style match program that sold for 10 euros. The popular European-style soccer scarves with Notre Dame and Navy logos are being hawked on the corners down Lansdowne Road.

Among the staff imported by CBS Sports for its telecast were a handful of Dutch photographers who had worked NFL Europe games and the NFL events at Wembley Stadium in London. About 35 production staffers came from the United States to assist in putting on the game.

And once the game started, Irish eyes (the Notre Dame version) kept smiling most of the afternoon. Notre Dame scored on its first three offensive possessions (first time that happened since the Nevada game in 2009), and that made it a relatively smooth first career start for Everett Golson at quarterback.

Notre Dame made more than enough plays to turn its ultra-long football road trip into a success story.

Running backs George Atkinson III and Theo Riddick both scored twice, defensive lineman Stephon Tuitt ran a recovered fumble back 77 yards for another score, and new quarterback Everett Golson eased into his new role effortlessly as the Irish rolled over Navy 50–10 at Aviva Stadium in Dublin, Ireland.

A sellout crowd of 48,820 fans looked on, and CBS televised the contest.

Notre Dame's overseas season opener might have been cause for concern for the Irish coaches—but 293 net rushing yards from Brian Kelly's squad, one harmless turnover, and a defense that limited the Middies' triple-option attack to 149 ground yards all contributed to a satisfying first time out.

The Irish made their first international venture since playing the same Navy team across town at Croke Park in 1996—and they sent the pro–Notre Dame crowd home with smiles on their faces.

Unranked Notre Dame displayed more than its share of offensive consistency in the opening half, scoring on drives of 75, 70, and 80 yards on its first three offensive possessions.

On his way to 107 rushing yards, Riddick capped the opening 11-play excursion with an 11-yard scoring run. Golson had 11-yard completions to both Riddick and TJ Jones on that opening attempt.

Everett Golson lets fly during his first start at quarterback for the Irish—Week 1 of the 2012 season in Dublin, Ireland vs. Navy.

Notre Dame linebacker Manti Te'o stopped Navy quarterback Trey Miller on a fourth-and-one play at the Irish 30. Then, after the Irish put one first down in the bank, Atkinson raced 56 yards to put Notre Dame up two scores.

Golson finished off a 10-play, 80-yard drive with a five-yard fade toss to tight end Tyler Eifert, with a 35-yard throw from Golson to DaVaris Daniels covering ground to the Navy 16 and eventually a 20–0 Irish lead.

Golson threw his lone interception, and Navy marched from its own 9 to the Irish 16. Then Tuitt's recovery and runback after a Miller bobble made it 27–0 with just over two minutes left in the opening half.

Navy connected for a 26-yard field goal as time ran out in the second period to cap a 72-yard march—and the Middies notched their lone touchdown less than a minute into the third period on a 25-yard throw from Miller to Shawn Lynch. It was all Irish from there.

Atkinson's three-yard TD rush finished off an 87-yard, 12-play drive—with a 29-yard Golson-to–Troy Niklas connection taking the Irish to the Middies 3. Riddick's second TD run from three yards out made it 40–10 after three periods, with a Cam McDaniel 19-yard run marking the big play of that possession. Atkinson finished with 99 rushing yards on his nine attempts.

Nick Tausch connected on a 34-yard field goal with six minutes left in the game, and Robby Toma closed the scoring in the final minute with a nine-yard run to end a 68-yard drive.

The Irish had 490 total yards, while Navy hurt itself with four turnovers, including three lost fumbles.

Golson may not have been spectacular, but he hit 12 of his 18 throws for 144 yards and the one interception. Tuitt made up for that miscue moments later with his fumble return. Eifert led Irish receivers with four grabs for 22 yards.

Te'o recorded his first career fumble recovery and first career interception to key the Irish defensive effort. Cornerback Bennett Jackson and linebacker Dan Fox each had seven tackles, while Te'o added six.

The Irish highlights included:

- Theo Riddick's 11-yard TD run in the first period marked the first rushing TD in his career (he has six on receptions).
- Notre Dame played 47 players in the first period, 14 of whom saw their first college action.
- George Atkinson III's 56-yarder marked the longest TD run by an Irish running back since Jonas Gray's 79-yarder at Pitt in 2011.
- KeiVarae Russell became the first Notre Dame freshman ever to start at cornerback.

Stephon Tuitt (7) recovers a Navy fumble before running it back 77 yards for a Notre Dame touchdown during a 50–10 victory for the Irish.

The Fighting Irish celebrate their victory over Navy in Dublin's Aviva Stadium.

Kelly was understandably satisfied after the 50–10 win. His Irish had taken on a different sort of challenge, handled all the variables, dealt with the nuances of life in a different country for a few days, and still won a football game handily.

First and foremost, you're playing an option team in Navy. We all know the history there. The year before we shut them down, but they beat us a few years back. So any time you open up with Navy, your defense is going to be tested.

I think we saw how good we could be defensively. We saw Stephon Tuitt come up with the big, dynamic play. And then Tyler Eifert—we saw that he was going to be a playmaker. So we got some glimpses of what the team could be like against a well-coached Navy team. But we really didn't know who we were until we got into the Big Ten schedule.

—Brian Kelly

I liked the plan for Everett's first game. Let's manage the game, and let's get him some confidence and do all we can to get him off to a good start. Let's get him some easy throws, run the ball, and take advantage of our physical size. That went according to plan. We know we're not going to beat everybody 50–10. But this was what we needed. Aesthetically, we didn't have turnovers. We didn't have penalties. We kind of flowed nicely.

—*Chuck Martin*

With the time difference, the Notre Dame charter flight ended up back in South Bend about midnight.

Tuesday, September 4

For all of the football and logistics that went according to plan in Dublin, it's only natural that the next question revolved around how the Irish players would respond physically to the international travel and whether it would have any effect on Game 2.

Brian Kelly was confident there were no issues:

- "I think everybody has talked about how our team will bounce back from the trip to Ireland. We had a great shakeout Monday. Our guys had good energy, and today we'll have a full two-hour practice…. We feel great. We think the plan that we have put in place over the long term has really worked out quite well, so we can focus strictly on playing the ballgame."
- "We respect Purdue. We know them as [a team] that's going to play great football against us, but our attention is on ourselves. And the attention focuses squarely on the things that we have to do better. We were pleased with the win against Navy, there's no question about that. We played the game that I wanted to play. We won it up front and we took care of the football by and large. The game plan for Navy was executed by our

players—and there will be a new game plan this week, and there will be one for Michigan State and Oklahoma and BYU. As we move through each week, we'll get challenged in different areas. That's why I respect Purdue, I respect Coach [Danny] Hope and the work that they have done. They are a bowl team from last year, a physical, Big Ten team. But really the focus for me as the head coach at Notre Dame is on our guys this week and what we have to improve upon, and as I mentioned, there's a number of areas that we have got to do a lot of work on this week to get ready for Purdue."

- "Oh, there's so many things that he [Everett Golson] has to improve upon, but they are items that we feel really confident that he already has a good grasp on and will continue to evolve, and then there are things that we have to continue to work on with him on a day-to-day basis. This is a process for Everett. This will be a continuation, a week-to-week growing as a quarterback. I guess what I like the most in the big-picture sense was his comfortable place out on the field. He did not seem overwhelmed at any time. He was extremely communicative when he got to the sideline. He could tell me what was going on. Those are all, big picture, good things, after Game 1."

- "[Overcoming adversity against Navy] goes to your leadership, especially the guys up front when you're looking at [Zack] Martin and [Chris] Watt and [Braxston] Cave and [Mike] Golic. Those guys have been there, done that. I think it says a lot about the maturity and the leadership that we have on the football team. And, certainly, we have built a lot of resolve over last few years, and our guys know that they are going to have to overcome. We talk about that every day, you're going to have to overcome some adversity. They took the challenge, and it was good to see."

- "It's all about our development this week as a football team going into Week 2. There are so many things that we have to do defensively, relative to getting back to traditional offensive sets and coverages and nickel and dime, and all those things. And, from an offensive standpoint, we are now playing a team that matches up more physically with us. There's so many other things that we have to bring to the table from an offensive standpoint. So we'll work on all of those things this week."

Saturday, September 8

A week removed from their Dublin excursion, the Irish showed their stuff in Notre Dame Stadium for the first time in 2012 against Purdue.

Irish quarterback Tommy Rees didn't even make the trip to Dublin, Ireland, for Notre Dame's season-opening victory. Yet he came off the bench late with the score tied in the Irish home opener and took Notre Dame 55 yards downfield in the final two minutes. That gave Kyle Brindza the chance to knock through a 27-yard field goal with seven seconds remaining to account for a 20–17 victory over Purdue at Notre Dame Stadium.

A sellout crowd of 80,795 watched, and NBC televised the game. The Irish start the season 2–0 for the first time in four years.

After a dominant rushing effort produced nearly 300 ground yards the week before, Notre Dame this time managed only 52 rushing yards on 36 attempts. Meanwhile, Everett Golson generally proved efficient in connecting on 21 of his 31 throws for 289 yards without an interception.

Notre Dame never trailed and led 17–7 after three periods. Purdue rebounded with a field goal three seconds into the final stanza, capping a nine-play, 56-yard Boilermaker possession.

After a Golson lost fumble (Notre Dame's only turnover of the afternoon), Purdue drove 15 yards for the tying points, culminating in a fourth-down, 15-yard touchdown pass from Caleb TerBush to Antavian Edison at the 2:12 juncture.

With Golson a bit shaken up and having trouble gripping the ball after the fumble, the Irish turned to Rees, and the junior, who started the final 12 games a year ago, delivered.

Rees hit three passes in his six attempts, connecting on one third down for 10 yards to veteran John Goodman, then on another third down for 21 more to Robby Toma.

Brindza succeeded on the three-point attempt as the 12-play drive epitomized the two-minute drill.

Coach Brian Kelly made it clear after the game that Golson would remain the starter next week at Michigan State, suggesting Rees simply became the best option based on time and score.

Golson threw to Tyler Eifert for 22 yards on the game's first play from scrimmage, but that possession ended in a punt. Notre Dame's second offensive march traversed 69 yards in 13 plays before Brindza missed a 40-yard field goal.

Golson notched his first career touchdown to begin the scoring late in the second period as the Irish marched 88 yards in 10 plays. Notre Dame's quarterback had completions of 30 yards to Troy Niklas and 41 to DaVaris Daniels.

Purdue tied it at the half, traversing 58 yards for a two-yard Edison TD catch from Robert Marve with nine seconds remaining in the first half. The Boilers kept that drive alive with an 11-yard pass to Crosby Wright on fourth-and-four at the Irish 41—and the next play featured a 16-yard Marve toss to O.J. Ross.

Twenty-second-ranked Notre Dame took the lead in the first five minutes of the third period, driving 66 yards in 10 plays. Golson's three-yard pass to TJ Jones put the Irish up 14–7. Golson and Eifert collaborated for completions of 22 and 25 yards two plays apart to set the Irish up at the Boilermakers 3.

Brindza's 30-yard field goal extended the margin to 17–7 less than two minutes later. That came after a Purdue possession lasted only two plays before a Bennett Jackson interception.

Manti Te'o's 10 tackles, plus nine from Zeke Motta and seven from Carlo Calabrese, paced Notre Dame's defense. Stephon Tuitt had a pair of sacks.

What was there to like about Notre Dame's 20–17 football victory over Purdue? Here you go:

- The Irish dominated time of possession (34:14 to 25:46) and rank 12th in the nation in that category.
- Notre Dame won the turnover battle again (forcing two interceptions while committing one fumble) and rank eighth in the nation in turnover margin.

Irish players sing the Notre Dame alma mater after their 20–17 victory over Purdue.

- On offense the Irish converted 11 of 19 on third down and rank fourth in the nation in third-down-conversion percentage.
- Notre Dame had four drives of at least 10 plays, and those resulted in one TD, two field goals, and one missed field goal.
- The Irish scored on three straight possessions surrounding halftime (two 10-play TD drives and a field-goal drive on a short field following an interception).
- Notre Dame's quarterbacks combined to complete 24 of 37 passes for 324 yards with one TD—completing passes to nine different players and with seven pass completions of at least 20 yards.
- Everett Golson completed 21 of 31 passes (.678) for 289 yards with one passing TD and one rushing TD (the second-most passing yards ever by a Notre Dame quarterback making his Notre Dame Stadium debut).

We were confident coming into that week against Purdue. But we learned quickly that our quarterback was just not ready to do everything yet. We couldn't execute at the level that we needed to. But, again, you know certain parts of your team have to step up, and our defense stepped up big that day.

We found a way to win games at the quarterback position mixing an experienced player in Tommy Rees coming off the bench with an inexperienced but dynamic player in Everett Golson, and it worked. I'd like to tell you that there was a detailed plan. All we knew is that we had a gamer in Everett and a kid who would be fine coming off the bench in Tommy, and that worked well for us.

We need to get our starter right, and our starter is Everett Golson. We wanted him to start it and finish it. But we were losing sleep over the fact that he wasn't there yet, and we had to get him there during the week of practice. That was not easy. Everett was also dealing with the trust issue—do the coaches really trust me? They keep going to Tommy Rees when we get in trouble.

So every week it was a building of trust with Everett. It really was his job. It was about learning from the mistakes he made the week before, but there was a sense of comfort going into Saturday that you knew you had Tommy Rees on your team. A lot of work was placed in trying to get the quarterback position solidified with Golson starting the game and finishing the game.

—*Brian Kelly*

- Tyler Eifert had a career-high 98 receiving yards on four catches (all four receptions were longer than 20 yards).
- DaVaris Daniels had four catches for 70 yards, including a 41-yard reception (all in the first half).
- Theo Riddick and Robby Toma each had four receptions—and Riddick added 47 rushing yards on 10 carries in the second half.

Everett was still experiencing his first games at Notre Dame, and the second week of his career, Tommy goes in for a two-minute drill, and so we're trying to explain and get Everett to understand. He didn't understand at first. He understands it now, but through five, six, seven weeks, he didn't always understand the back and forth. But he was professional about it. I think he handled it awesome for where he was, being so young.

We were still trying to figure it out—I mean, obviously, we didn't chart the course of these 12 games. We're still learning our football team. Theo Riddick had such a major impact in the season. Whereas, last year in the middle of spring ball, did anybody think he would be a go-to tailback? You've got some guys in new spots and you've got a new quarterback, and you're still trying to learn how it's all going to work.

—*Chuck Martin*

- On defense the Irish permitted 288 total yards vs. Purdue after the Boiler-makers had 547 yards the previous week.

- Notre Dame limited Purdue to 6-of-17 on third down and allowed only 90 rushing yards on 30 carries.
- The Irish second-half defense: 109 total yards, eight total possessions that resulted in four three-and-outs, two interceptions, one sustained drive that led to a field goal, and one TD that occurred on a short field following an Everett Golson fumble.
- Purdue rushed 11 times for only 16 yards in the second half and was just 7-of-16 passing for 93 yards, with one TD and two interceptions.
- Purdue was 0-for-6 on third down in the second half.
- The Notre Dame first-team defense has allowed only one third-down conversion on nine attempts in the second half this season.
- Manti Te'o led the team with 10 tackles and added one quarterback hurry. Stephon Tuitt posted four tackles, two sacks, two tackles for loss, and two quarterback hurries (becoming the first Notre Dame player with at least two sacks in consecutive games since 2006).
- Bennett Jackson notched the first two interceptions of his career (the first interception led to a field goal and the second finished the game).
- On special teams, Kyle Brindza made two of three field goals, including the game-winner.
- Ben Turk hit punts of 50 and 53 yards.

An easy key to Notre Dame's 2–0 football record so far? Lack of turnovers. A year ago after two games, the Irish had committed 10 turnovers. This year? Only two—one interception thrown against Navy and one lost fumble against Purdue. Last year at this time, Notre Dame already was minus-7 in the turnover column—compared to plus-4 as of today.

You've heard plenty already about Notre Dame's football schedule challenges for 2012—so now the Irish will face five ranked opponents among their next six games, in meeting No. 10 Michigan State, No. 17 Michigan, No. 21 Stanford, No. 25 BYU, and then No. 5 Oklahoma (all rankings from Week 2's AP poll). The final game of the regular season is against then No. 2–rated USC.

Wednesday, September 12

The biggest news today came from Chapel Hill, North Carolina, where the Atlantic Coast Conference announced that the University of Notre Dame would become its newest member. While most Irish sports would play on a full-fledged basis (hockey will be joining Hockey East in 2013–2014), the decision to leave the Big East will have a significant impact on football. The new relationship will involve Notre Dame playing five football games per year against ACC opponents, starting with the 2014 season. Even more importantly, beginning in 2014 Notre Dame will have full access to the entire lineup of bowls connected to the ACC. That will solve the problem in which, in the current four-year rotation (2010–2013 regular seasons), Notre Dame's only option beyond qualifying for a Bowl Championship Series game is to play once in four years in the Champs Sports Bowl in Orlando. Since the Irish used up that option after the 2011 season, the 2012 and 2013 seasons essentially became BCS-or-bust scenarios for Brian Kelly's program. From a football standpoint, the Irish traded five games per year for the ability to have a viable list of bowl options on an ongoing basis. Still, Notre Dame retained its football independence, with the five ACC games likely to be joined by USC, Stanford, and Navy on an ongoing basis on future Irish schedules.

Today is a great day for the University of Notre Dame and our athletics department, including the football program. Speaking strictly from a football standpoint, we have further solidified our future as an independent in college football, maintained our unique ability to schedule nationally, and greatly improved our postseason bowl game options. I applaud [University president] Father [John] Jenkins and [athletics director] Jack Swarbrick for this move. They have set our entire athletics department up for great success in the future.

—*Brian Kelly*

Notre Dame athletics director Jack Swarbrick remarked: "I think this relationship worked so well because important needs were served to the benefit of both parties. We believe that our inclusion will help the ACC access better bowl games. It already has a great bowl package, but we think this can enhance it even more.

"For us, being part of the ACC gives us an assurance we can't find in the postseason bowl world as it is structured now—without some partner, some conference partner, to help you do it.

"If we finish in the top four, we know where we are going to be; if we finish slightly below that, we are going to have an opportunity in the Orange Bowl or one of the other host bowls—and below that, we are going to be in the ACC package. That's what we needed. We needed a soup-to-nuts solution for postseason, and we have achieved it."

Saturday, September 15

Whatever you wanted to make of Notre Dame's 2–0 start, this was a whole new challenge. Its first true road game. Against the 10th-ranked team in the country. Against an old Irish rival. In an emotional prime-time setting on national television. How would Brian Kelly's squad respond?

Notre Dame played turnover-free football, and quarterback Everett Golson took another step forward in his growth as the 20th-ranked Irish ended Michigan State's 15-game home-field win streak with a 20–3 win over the 10th-rated and unbeaten Spartans at Spartan Stadium in East Lansing, Michigan.

ABC televised the contest in prime time, as a capacity crowd of 79,219 fans looked on.

Off to its first 3–0 start in 10 years, the Irish limited Michigan State to 50 net rushing yards in recording their first victory over a top 10 opponent in seven seasons. It marked the biggest Spartan loss at home since a 20–3 defeat to Central Michigan in 1991.

Golson ran for one score and threw for another as Notre Dame let its defense dominate the field-position battle against a Michigan State defense that hadn't allowed a touchdown in either of its first two outings.

In his first appearance in an opponent's stadium, Golson eluded the Spartans and threw across the grain to find John Goodman in the end zone for a 36-yard touchdown play on Notre Dame's second possession, less than five minutes into the opening period.

Brian Kelly's crew had held the Spartans to a three-and-out on the initial Michigan State drive, with Notre Dame taking over on its own 49 after a punt. Golson completed a 14-yard throw to Robby Toma, then found Goodman two plays later. The Spartans missed a 44-yard field-goal attempt after driving 49 yards later in the opening period. The Irish defense notched three second-period sacks, and the first of those forced a punt that set up Notre Dame near midfield.

George Atkinson III scampered 32 yards on first down, and two plays later a Golson-to–TJ Jones connection for 14 yards put the Irish at the Michigan State 4. Golson finally ran six yards for a 14–0 advantage less than five minutes into the second period.

Michigan State's only points of the night came on the following Spartans drive. That 13-play, 43-yard, seven-minute possession ended in a 50-yard Dan Conroy field goal.

Notre Dame players celebrate their 20–3 win over Michigan State in the locker room with the Megaphone Trophy, awarded to the winner of the Irish-Spartans game since 1949.

Neither team seriously threatened in the third period, as the Irish and Spartans accounted for six punts, three by each squad, and six combined first downs. Michigan State reached its own 49, and Notre Dame hit the midfield mark—but that's as far as either team could advance in that quarter.

Notre Dame controlled the football for nearly seven minutes on one final-period possession. The 84-yard, 11-play drive featured a 26-yard rush by Cierre Wood and an eight-yard Wood run on a fourth-and-one opportunity. Kyle Brindza finished off that sequence with a 29-yard field goal for a 17–3 lead at the 6:21 mark.

When Spartans standout running back Le'Veon Bell (he had 77 rushing yards on 19 carries) attempted a lateral that Manti Te'o grabbed, Brindza ended the scoring with a 47-yard field goal with three minutes and 18 seconds to go.

Golson finished with 14 completions on 32 attempts for 178 yards, while Michigan State's Andrew Maxwell converted 23 of 45 for 187.

The Irish trio of Wood, Atkinson, and Theo Riddick combined on 27 rushing attempts for 129 yards.

Te'o finished with a dozen tackles, and Prince Shembo had nine (one of them a sack).

Bell had only four second-half rushing attempts for 13 yards, as Notre Dame's lead forced the Spartans to the air. Michigan State's normally robust run game managed only three net yards on six tries in the final two periods.

There were plenty of nifty accomplishments in Notre Dame's 20–3 road win against 10th-rated Michigan State in East Lansing:

- The Irish won the turnover battle for the third straight game.
- Subtract four kneel-downs for minus-14 yards, and Notre Dame rushed 30 times for 136 yards (4.5 yards per carry) against one of the best defenses in the country.
- On the critical fourth-quarter possession that resulted in a 29-yard field goal, the drive went for 84 yards and took 6:35 off the game clock, as the Irish rushed nine times for 69 yards (7.7 yards per carry), including 45 yards on five rushes for Cierre Wood.

I think the Michigan State game for us was, more than anything else, a defining moment in that we had to play the game the way that I had wanted to play it the first couple of years. That was a physical and mental toughness and kind of exerting our will against our opponent. It was the first time against a top-ranked team that we exerted our will. We were physically stronger; we were mentally tougher, and that was kind of the mindset going in. The football team really responded in that big moment. I think we gained an understanding not only of the way that I wanted to play the game in 2012, but also of the confidence we took from going on the road to beat Michigan State.

—Brian Kelly

- Notre Dame took advantage of two short-field opportunities in the first half with two TD drives of 51 yards.
- The Irish possessed the ball for 18:32 of the second half, despite going 0-for-9 on third down.
- Entering the game, Michigan State was one of two FBS teams that hadn't allowed an offensive TD. Notre Dame scored two offensive TDs in its first five possessions of the game.

You go to Michigan State on the road, and obviously it's a huge test. At that point I think coach [Kelly] knew that, if we don't give up big plays, our defense is pretty salty up front. But the Michigan State game proved that against a physical team on the road that traditionally gives Notre Dame fits. We won the big battle in the trenches on defense, and we won enough of the battles on offense.

I think coach also saw that, hey, this physical football team is now starting to work. Our front seven on defense controlled the line of scrimmage, and they might complete some short passes. But if we can get after the quarterback enough we've got a good chance. Then offensively in the fourth quarter, we went on a seven-minute drive against a really good defense.

What we've been trying to do since January just helped us win a football game on the road against a very good team. Everett [Golson] played well, which is another plus, and Everett got huge confidence from that game. So it's a lot of positives coming out of Michigan State.

Coming back to prepare for Michigan, in the kids' minds, we had talked about physicality. We watched the fourth quarter against Michigan State, and the whole group's starting to buy in, looking at how our defense played in the trenches. Looking at how our offense played, particularly as the game wore on—we're getting stronger, not weaker. It's all the conditioning we're talking about, playing four quarters of success and finishing strong.

So all of coach's four quarters success played out at Michigan State. It's everything he talks about to win football games. You watch the game, and there I saw all of those things he's been talking about for three years.

—*Chuck Martin*

- The Irish defense allowed 237 total yards on 70 plays (3.4 yards/play) to a team that had been averaging 478 yards/game and 5.7 yards/play.
- Notre Dame allowed only 50 rushing yards on 25 carries (2.0 yards/carry) to a team averaging 193 rushing yards/game and 4.2 yards/carry.
- Over the last two years combined, Notre Dame has allowed only 79 combined rushing yards vs. Michigan State on 48 carries (1.6 yards/carry).
- Michigan State never reached the red zone and only had one snap out of 33 plays in the second half occur in Notre Dame territory (the Notre Dame 48 was the deepest Michigan State got in second half).
- The Irish held Le'Veon Bell to 77 rushing yards on 19 carries and took him out of the game in the second half as he only recorded four carries after the halftime break (only one rush gained more than seven yards).

- Michigan State entered the game rushing the ball 55 percent of the time but rushed it only 35 percent of the time against Notre Dame.
- The three points allowed were the fewest Michigan State had scored in a home game since 1991.
- The Irish defense has allowed 30 total points in its first three games combined—the fewest points allowed in the first three games of a season since 1988.
- Manti Te'o led the team with 12 tackles, one tackle for loss, one fumble recovery, and two pass breakups (Te'o was named Walter Camp National Defensive Player of the Week for his efforts).
- Prince Shembo had a career-high nine tackles (tying his previous high with eight in the first half alone), including two tackles for loss, one sack, and two quarterback hurries.
- The Irish defensive line combined for 23 tackles, $3^1/_2$ sacks, $4^1/_2$ tackles for loss, and five quarterback hurries.
- On special teams, Ben Turk landed four of eight punts inside the 20 and averaged 42.4 on those eight kicks.
- Turk's second-half punts traveled 53 yards (downed at the Michigan State 12), 50, 46 (downed at the Spartans' 4), and 35—flipping the field on three of those four punts.
- He also generated a personal foul after Michigan State failed to block his punt.
- Kyle Brindza converted both field goals from 29 and 47 yards—and four of five kickoffs went for touchbacks.

Notre Dame outgained Michigan State 189 to 121 yards in the first half despite the fact the Spartans won the time of possession battle by 17:52 to 12:08. Michigan State had only 47 rushing yards in the first 30 minutes, and 15 came on a meaningless final play of the half.

Michigan State did not allow a sack in either of its first two games, but Notre Dame had three by halftime.

Notre Dame's first-period TD pass (Everett Golson to John Goodman) marked the first offensive TD allowed by Michigan State this year in three games.

The next challenge? The Irish next Saturday night against Michigan will attempt to defeat ranked opponents on consecutive Saturdays for the first time since 2005 (at Pittsburgh and at Michigan in Charlie Weis' first two games as Notre Dame head coach).

Monday, September 17

After three weekends of play, the Irish stand eighth nationally in scoring defense (10.0 points per game), 10th in sacks (3.67), 11th in turnover margin (plus-1.67), 17th in net punting (40.73), 18th in total defense (288.67 yards), 23rd in rushing defense (96.33 yards) and 26th in pass efficiency defense (106.24 rating). Individually, Stephon Tuitt is tied for third in sacks at 1.67 per game.

Meanwhile, Michigan is ranked 12th in pass defense (157.67 yards per game) and 13th in sacks allowed (.67). Wolverines quarterback Denard Robinson ranks ninth individually in total offense per game (350 yards) and 18th in rushing (117 yards).

You don't need to say much when Michigan comes to Notre Dame Stadium, but given the things Robinson has accomplished against the Irish the last two years, the matchup between him and the Notre Dame defense figures to earn top billing.

Tuesday, September 18

If the game wasn't enough, 62 members of the 1977 Notre Dame national championship football team are returning to campus this weekend for their 35th reunion. That team will be honored on the field Saturday just prior to the game.

In addition, the national colors will be presented Saturday by former Notre Dame head football coach Ara Parseghian and his wife, Katie, in recognition of Notre Dame's celebration this season of 125 years of football (1887–2012). Ara led the Irish from 1964 to 1974, won consensus national titles in 1966 and 1973, and is a member of the College Football Hall of Fame.

If you are looking for a little more color and pageantry, streets in both South Bend and Mishawaka were renamed Fighting Irish Drive this morning in separate ceremonies involving the mayors of both cities (Pete Buttigieg in South Bend, Dave Wood in Mishawaka). The South

Former Fighting Irish head football coach Ara Parseghian (center) presents the stars and stripes prior to the Notre Dame–Michigan game at Notre Dame Stadium.

Bend change took place at the corner of Michigan and Washington Streets, the Mishawaka version at the corner of Main and Douglas. The name changes are in honor of Notre Dame's celebration of 125 years of football.

Interestingly enough, the Notre Dame–Michigan game Saturday night marks the 30th anniversary, almost to the day, of the first night game ever played at Notre Dame Stadium in 1982 (also against Michigan). Since night games in Notre Dame's home facility have become a bit rarer in recent decades, this one figures to earn its share of attention.

Mike Golic Jr. today was one of 22 college football players named to the 2012 All-State AFCA Good Works Team. The Good Works Team recognizes the positive, off-the-field impact that a select group of student-athletes has on their communities. Golic participated in a fundraiser for St. Baldrick's Foundation for childhood cancer research that raised approximately $160,000 over the last four years. He also served as a counselor in the Irish Experience League in 2011 and 2012, when 40 local kids came to Notre Dame's campus to interact with Irish student-athletes. At last year's pediatric Christmas party—an event where kids in local hospitals came to Notre Dame's campus for a party with Irish student-athletes—Golic dressed as Santa Claus. Notre Dame has had a handful of its players named to this team over the years, and they understand there's more to being a student-athlete than just what goes on between the lines.

Friday, September 21

The Notre Dame–Michigan pep rally was held on an overcast evening on the Library Mall, in the area north of Notre Dame Stadium and south of the Hesburgh Library. Tight end Troy Niklas grabbed everyone's attention when he took off his shirt as the punchline to his remarks—but what the fans remembered was Manti Te'o struggling to keep his emotions in check as those in attendance paid tribute to him as he returned for his first home game following the loss of his grandmother.

Saturday, September 22

For the second year in a row, Notre Dame played one night game at home at Notre Dame Stadium—and in 2012 it was Michigan that came to town for the evening affair.

Notre Dame finally found a way to stop elusive Michigan quarterback Denard Robinson, in the process providing the best indication yet that the 2012 Irish defense may be for real, based on the first month of the college football season.

The 11th-rated Irish moved to 4–0 thanks to a 13–6 win over 18th-ranked Michigan in a prime-time outing at Notre Dame Stadium. The Irish defense intercepted Robinson four times in the first half alone, then recovered a Robinson fumble on the first possession of the second half. Over one stretch in the first half, Notre Dame intercepted five consecutive Wolverines pass attempts, including one by running back Vincent Smith.

With 80,795 fans packing the Irish home facility, NBC televised the action.

The Michigan defeat marked its eighth straight on the road against ranked opponents dating to 2006—while the Irish rebounded after three straight seasons of falling to Michigan when the Wolverines scored in the final 27 seconds.

After Robinson rolled up 948 combined total yards of offense in last-minute Michigan wins over the Irish the past two seasons, this time Notre Dame held a Big Ten opponent without a touchdown for a second straight week.

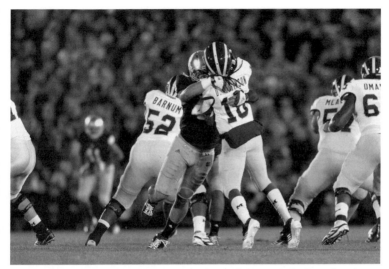

The Irish defense sacks Wolverines quarterback Denard Robinson during Notre Dame's 13–6 victory over Michigan in Week 4.

Notre Dame's own offense didn't earn high marks, notching just 239 total yards, only 94 on the ground. For the second time in two home games, quarterback Tommy Rees came off the bench to lead the Irish to victory.

Robinson finished with a team-leading 90 rushing yards on 26 carries, and he threw for 138 yards on 13-of-24 accuracy. But Michigan never found the end zone and didn't score at all until a pair of fourth-period field goals by Brendan Gibbons.

Notre Dame's Manti Te'o played a key role, intercepting two passes, forcing a fumble, and making eight tackles.

Though neither team scored in the opening period, the Wolverines dominated the quarter, holding the football for more than 11 minutes.

Golson threw an interception on Notre Dame's first play from scrimmage, with Michigan's Gibbons missing a field goal from 43 yards out on the resulting possession.

The Wolverines next traveled from their own 12 to the Irish 10 on 12 plays over more than six minutes, but Smith's first-and-goal throw ended up in the hands of Irish freshman Nicky Baratti in the end zone.

A second consecutive Michigan possession ended in an interception, this one coming on a third-and-11 Wolverines play. This time it was Te'o who grabbed a Robinson throw and returned it to the Michigan 17. From there, Kyle Brindza booted a 33-yarder at the 10:09 mark for Notre Dame's first points.

Robinson threw another pick on the very next play—with Bennett Jackson bringing it back to the Wolverines 39. The Irish returned the favor less than two minutes later. Golson completed passes to Theo Riddick for 13 yards and DaVaris Daniels for 16, but Golson's second-and-goal attempt from the 10 ended up in the hands of Michigan's Thomas Gordon in the end zone.

Robinson ran it three straight times for a combined 14 yards, then on second-and-seven, Te'o added a second interception. From the Michigan 48, the Irish needed eight plays, with Rees now at the helm, for their lone touchdown of the night. A 24-yard completion from Rees to TJ Jones on third-and-five at the Michigan 30 marked Notre Dame's biggest play. Rees accounted for the TD on first-and-goal from the 2, making it 10–0 with 1:21 left in the half.

Robinson ran twice, then threw his fourth interception on four second-period possessions, with Irish rookie KeiVarae Russell returning the pickoff 31 yards as the half ended.

Michigan ran for 40 yards in the second quarter but had all four of its pass attempts intercepted as the Irish held the football for 9:42.

The Wolverines' initial third-period possession lasted 71 yards—until Danny Spond forced a Robinson fumble that Jackson recovered at the Irish 8-yard line. Notre Dame ran off only seven plays in the third period for 29 yards.

Michigan drove from its own 43 to the Irish 15 late in the third and early in the fourth period—with Gibbons getting the visitors on the board with his 33-yard field goal with 13:10 remaining in the game for a 10–3 Irish lead.

Notre Dame bounced back with its own three-pointer—Brindza capped a 53-yard possession with a 39-yarder that made it 13–3 at the 6:46 juncture. Riddick ran seven times on the drive and also caught a pass.

The Wolverines made it a one-possession game with their own 11-play, 56-yard drive that went as far as the Irish 14 before Gibbons converted a 31-yard field goal with 3:27 left.

From there Notre Dame managed to run out the clock, going from its own 25-yard line all the way to the Michigan 21 when time expired. Rees found Eifert for 38 yards on a huge third-and-four conversion from the Notre Dame 31.

Here's the best and the brightest from Notre Dame's 13–6 win over Michigan on Saturday night:

- The Irish finished plus-4 in turnover margin, as for the first time in 10 years Notre Dame beat top 20 opponents in consecutive weeks.
- The Notre Dame offense did not allow a sack.
- Tommy Rees came off the bench to hit eight of 11 throws for 115 yards—and the offense did not commit a turnover after he entered.
- The Irish totaled 99 yards of offense on 17 plays in the fourth quarter (5.8 yards per play), after only 140 yards on 33 plays through three quarters (4.2 yards per play).

- Notre Dame's two fourth-quarter drives: 11 plays for 53 yards in 6:24, resulting in a field goal, then seven plays for 51 yards that ran the last 3:27 off the clock.

Denard Robinson was everything we thought he would be. But we knew we had to force him to throw the football. We were able to have some success on first down, get in a position where they had to throw the ball. And we felt that, if we could force Michigan to throw, we had an opportunity to be successful. Obviously, the number of interceptions we had put us in a position to win. The only problem was we were shooting ourselves in the foot left and right offensively, as well. That was one of those games where we won the game despite ourselves. We lost so many opportunities. We had to go and take Everett [Golson] out of the game. Tommy [Rees] came in, and, again, we just found a way to grind one out.

—*Brian Kelly*

- The Irish defense forced six turnovers: five interceptions—four thrown by Denard Robinson, one by Vincent Smith (the most picks in a game for a Notre Dame defense since 1988 vs. Purdue)—and one fumble.
- Notre Dame actually intercepted five consecutive pass attempts by Michigan in the first half—potentially an all-time college football record—and forced turnovers on six consecutive possessions.
- Notre Dame's eight combined interceptions this season (through four games) equals the total number of Irish interceptions for the 2011 season.
- The 13 turnovers forced is one short of the 2011 total (only one team in the country has generated more turnovers in 2012).
- The Irish did not allow Michigan a TD despite five trips to the red zone (two field goals, one interception, one fumble, and one missed field goal).

- Notre Dame allowed only two field goals to Michigan (the fewest points scored in a game by the Wolverines since 2007), marking the first time since 1943 Notre Dame has allowed six points or less to top 20 opponents in consecutive weeks.
- The Irish defense has not allowed a touchdown in its last eight quarters and has allowed a total of only three TDs in its four games this year.
- The 36 points allowed through the first four games are the fewest points allowed at this point of an Irish season since 1975 (Notre Dame ranks fourth in FBS in scoring defense, allowing nine points per game).
- Notre Dame held Denard Robinson to his lowest quarterback rating as a starting quarterback: he was 13-of-24 for 138 yards and four interceptions. After totaling 969 yards of total offense against Notre Dame the last two years, he was held to 228 yards this time.
- Bennett Jackson had a career-high nine tackles and added one interception and one fumble recovery
- Danny Spond contributed seven tackles and forced one fumble in the red zone, recovered by Jackson.

You go to the Michigan game, and, obviously, our defense is playing great early. But we're playing about as poorly on offense as Michigan's offense is playing. Their defense is giving the ball to us, and we're giving the ball to them. It's like a Ping-Pong match. Everett didn't have a good day, and we had no explanation.

So Tommy [Rees] comes in and does a great job again. This time Tommy plays two and a half quarters, and it goes right down to the last drive when he takes the knee.

He completes a huge ball in the fourth quarter. He has Tyler Eifert down the sideline, and it puts energy in the whole stadium and gives us more belief. So, no matter how it happened, we just beat Michigan and Michigan State back to back. It's hard for anyone, and it's been tough for Notre Dame. But we're 4–0.

—Chuck Martin

Sunday, September 23

College football fans are taking notice of the Irish. NBC Sports' presentation of Michigan–Notre Dame football was watched by 6.4 million viewers, allowing NBC to win the night in prime time and making the contest the most-watched Notre Dame prime-time game ever on NBC, as well as the most-watched Fighting Irish game on the broadcast network in more than two years. It was the most-watched Notre Dame game on NBC since the last time the Wolverines came to Notre Dame Stadium two seasons ago (7 million viewers on September 11, 2010). Notre Dame–Michigan was NBC's top-rated non-Olympic Saturday since the night of the Detroit Lions–New Orleans Saints NFL Wild-Card game on January 7, 2012.

The only schools in the country so far this year that have not given up a rushing score are Notre Dame, South Carolina, Nebraska, and TCU. The Irish have allowed only three combined TDs to their four opponents—and the only teams to allow fewer offensive TDs are TCU (one) and Cincinnati (two). Notre Dame also did not allow a rushing TD in its last two games of 2011, so the Irish have gone six straight games overall without giving up a ground score. The last time Notre Dame went four straight games in the same season without allowing a rushing TD was 1992 (October 10 vs. Pittsburgh, October 24 vs. BYU, October 31 vs. Navy, and November 7 vs. Boston College). The last time the Irish began a season without permitting a rushing TD in four straight games to start a season was 1989 (no offensive rushing TDs in the first five games).

Monday, September 24

With an open date this week, this will be a more low-key period of workouts for the Irish, with some time off for the players on the weekend.

Meanwhile, word comes that *Sports Illustrated* this week will include a feature on Notre Dame football linebacker Manti Te'o—with Te'o appearing on a regional edition cover.

This comes courtesy of ESPN.com's Ivan Maisel: "Notre Dame senior linebacker Manti Te'o has five turnovers, more than 19 FBS teams, including Michigan (four) and No. 17 Oklahoma (somehow, only one). The Fighting Irish have forced 13 turnovers this season, one fewer than in all of 2011. And Notre Dame has allowed only two touchdowns in 10 red zone trips (20 percent). Last season, opponents scored 25 touchdowns in 43 trips (58 percent). So that's why the No. 9 Irish are 4–0."

We're working all the time to win close games in the fall. We're working for kids to be able to handle not only adversity but adjustments. We may have two different guys back there at quarterback. But, if we have a problem, are we going to blame it on the fact that there is a different guy putting his hand under center? Whatever happens here, we're going to keep pushing forward. There's a constant daily reminder that it's not always perfect. And that's okay that it's not perfect yet. But can we win this Saturday not being perfect?

We'd love to have everything just how the world wants it to be. I'm not sure anyone's ever done what we've done with two quarterbacks. Now a guy's gotten hurt, and another guy has handled the rest of the game. No one's had what we did for 12 weeks. We managed all of those emotions, and we kept getting better on both sides of the ball. Our guys managed that and focused on what we had to focus on. There are a lot of great moments, but there were a lot of times when we've got to be better. We're not a finished product. But can we win not being a finished product? We were able to do that.

—Chuck Martin

Chapter 6

October

Monday, October 1

When Irish athletics officials came up with the concept of the "off-site home" game as it's named (call it a neutral-site game or a game that could be played in Notre Dame Stadium that's moved to another location), the idea was to go places Notre Dame doesn't normally play football. Thus San Antonio, Yankee Stadium, FedEx Field.

But, with Chicago boasting the most Notre Dame alumni (and fans?) of any city in the country, it became hard to ignore the idea of playing at Soldier Field, site of USC's first Midwest football visits to play the Irish in 1927 and 1929. And, what better way to do it than rekindling a rivalry from a few decades back—with the first regular season meeting between the Irish and Miami since 1990.

The Notre Dame athletics administration invited a handful of Notre Dame alums involved in Chicago sports to attend: Brooks Boyer, CMO, Chicago White Sox; Stan Bowman, VP/GM, Chicago Blackhawks; Ted Phillips, president, Chicago Bears; John Paxson, vice president, Chicago Bulls; Crane Kenney, president, Chicago Cubs; Scott Paddock, president, Chicagoland Speedway; Pat Salvi, owner, Gary Railcats/U.S. Steel Yard; Ruth Riley, Chicago Sky; Jeff Samardzija, Chicago Cubs. Chicago native Chris Zorich made an appearance on set for the Irish website pregame show, as did former Bengal Bout star and current professional boxer Mike Lee, another Chicagoan.

Tuesday, October 2

Here's this week's look at Notre Dame football by the numbers:

10. Notre Dame has 10 players on its roster from the Chicago area, more players than from any other metropolitan area.

9. Notre Dame's defense ranks ninth in the NCAA Football Bowl Subdivision (FBS) in both sacks (3.5/game) and pass efficiency defense (96.79 rating).

8. The Irish defense has totaled eight interceptions in 2012. That total is equal to the number of interceptions the 2011 Notre Dame defense recorded in 13 games. Only three schools are averaging more interceptions per game than the Irish.

7. Manti Te'o has played a role in seven of the 13 turnovers forced by Notre Dame's defense. The All-America linebacker has recorded three interceptions, recovered two fumbles, and hurried passers on two occasions that resulted in interceptions.

6. Junior cornerback Bennett Jackson and Te'o are each tied for sixth in the FBS in interceptions per game with three picks in four contests.

5. The five takeaways this year by senior linebacker Manti Te'o are equal to the turnovers accumulated by the defenses of No. 14 Oregon State (four) and No. 17 Oklahoma (one)—combined.

4. The 36 points allowed through the first four games are the fewest by a Notre Dame defense through an opening four games since the 1975

Irish defense permitted 20 points. This year's Notre Dame defense ranks third in the FBS in scoring defense at nine points per game.

3. Notre Dame ranks third in the FBS in turnover margin as the Irish are plus-9 through four games in that category. For comparison's sake, through four games in 2011, the Irish ranked 120th in the FBS and were minus-10 in turnover margin.

2. Notre Dame's defense ranks second in the FBS in lowest percentage of touchdowns allowed on red zone trips. Irish opponents have only scored two touchdowns in 10 trips to the red zone this year.

1. The Irish are the one team in the FBS to have not trailed in any game this year. It's the first time since 1989 that a Notre Dame team has not trailed in any of the first four games to open a season.

0. Zero rushing touchdowns have been scored against Notre Dame's defense this year. The Irish are the only team in the FBS to have not permitted a rushing score in 2012.

Friday, October 5

It's a busy day for Irish fans, beginning with a luncheon at Navy Pier featuring coach Brian Kelly and former Irish standouts Tony Rice and Pat Terrell (both now living in Chicago), who qualified as yesteryear stars of Notre Dame–Miami battles. Other guests of honor at Kelly's table included Irish stars John Lattner, the Heisman Trophy winner from Chicago, and Terry Brennan, a former Notre Dame standout running back who became a legend as a high school coach in the Chicago Catholic League before coming to coach at Notre Dame from 1954 to 1958.

The Irish bused from South Bend during the afternoon and made a quick practice stop at a windy, chilly Soldier Field.

Rice and Terrell did double duty at the Friday night pep rally held at Millennium Park. A contingent of former Lou Holtz players, many of whom played against the Hurricanes in the '80s, held their own reunion and dinner at a downtown location.

Saturday, October 6

Historic Soldier Field became a friendly prime-time home for the Notre Dame football program.

Miami threw a few early scares into the Irish under the Soldier Field lights, with a couple of long throws that barely missed connections. Notre Dame responded by holding yet another opponent without a touchdown—while showcasing a dominant, clock-eating, second-half rushing attack to maintain the football.

The first regular-season renewal of one of the most noteworthy college football rivalries of the late 1980s and early '90s proved rather one-sided in a prime-time matchup at Soldier Field in Chicago.

Ninth-ranked and undefeated Notre Dame made great use of a nearly unstoppable running game to wallop Miami 41–3, with George Atkinson III (10 carries for 123 yards) and Cierre Wood (18 for 118) leading the charge. It marked the first Irish running back tandem to both eclipse the 100-yard mark in a decade.

A full house of 62,871 fans looked on as NBC televised the game, with Notre Dame advancing to 5–0.

The Irish scored on their first three offensive possessions, though the margin at the half was only 13–3. Notre Dame rolled over the Hurricanes at will most of the second half, ending with a final possession time of more than 39 minutes.

Brian Kelly's squad scored four second-half TDs all on the ground (two by Wood, one 55-yarder by Atkinson, and one by Cam McDaniel). That quartet of scoring excursions comprised 81, 86, 66, and 93 yards for a combined 326 yards on Notre Dame's only second-half drives.

Former Fighting Irish star halfback and Heisman Trophy winner John Lattner performs the coin coss prior to kickoff of the Notre Dame–Miami game at Soldier Field in Chicago.

In holding a third straight opponent without a TD, the Irish dodged a couple of early bullets when the 'Canes misfired on several potential big-gaining pass plays. Miami had averaged 43 points and 630 yards in its previous two games.

On the other side of the ball, Irish quarterback Everett Golson rebounded with his most proficient outing yet, completing six straight passes to start the game and finishing 17-of-22 for 186 yards. Golson displayed his rushing skills for the first time on an extensive basis, running six times for 51 yards.

He played a major role in Notre Dame's 587 total yards and its best rushing total in a dozen seasons. Two-hundred seventy of the Irish rushing yards came after halftime.

Miami's only points came 10 minutes into the opening period on a 28-yard Jake Wieclaw field goal that ended a 50-yard drive. Miami moved as far as the Irish 7 late in the game, on its best chance for a TD, but handed the ball back on downs.

Neither team turned the ball over. The Irish ran off 77 plays to 53 for Miami.

Notre Dame linebacker Manti Te'o notched 10 tackles, with freshman cornerback KeiVarae Russell adding six.

Notre Dame's opening possession lasted 10 plays and 88 yards. The Irish benefitted from a roughing-the-kicker penalty on an attempted Notre Dame punt, plus another personal foul. Theo Riddick ventured the final yard for the 7–0 lead at the 9:28 mark. Miami drove back those 50 yards to the Irish 11 for the Wieclaw three-pointer that turned out to be the 'Canes lone points of the evening.

The Irish came right back with an impressive 70-yard, 12-play possession that featured a 15-yard Golson rush and a Golson-to–Tyler Eifert pass play for 23. After reaching the Miami 5, Brindza converted a 22-yard field goal. After a Hurricanes punt, Notre Dame came up with another seven-minute drive—going 65 yards before another Brindza field goal, this time from 32 yards out.

Both teams missed field goals on their last first-half possessions— the Irish from 34 yards as time expired after marching 53 yards to the Miami 17.

The Irish recorded 10 first downs and 135 yards in the second period alone but had only the pair of field goals to show for their work.

Hardly anything went wrong for the Irish after the halftime break. Wood's 37-yard run set up his two-yard TD rush on the following play for a 20–3 Irish lead. Notre Dame's next scoring march featured 12 straight running plays for 86 yards. Atkinson's 31-yarder marked the largest gain on that series. The Atkinson 55-yard TD dash made it 34–3 with 23 seconds left in the third period.

Miami's best shot at a TD came in the final period—but the 'Canes 78-yard attempt ended at the Irish 7 when Stephen Morris' fourth-down pass went awry.

Notre Dame attempted only three second-half passes, completing them all.

McDaniel finished off the scoring with a one-yard run on third-and-goal to conclude a 13-play, 93-yard possession that lasted 8:45 and ran the Irish advantage to 38 points.

That final drive began with an 18-yard Atkinson run and also included a seven-yard gain by McDaniel on fourth-and-five, another McDaniel run for 15, plus a Tommy Rees–to–McDaniel completion for 21. If you missed the 41–3 Irish victory over Miami, here were the highlights:

- Notre Dame now is the only team in the nation to have not trailed in any game this season. It's the first time a Notre Dame team has not trailed in each of the first five games of a season since the 1947 national championship team.
- This marks the first five-game winning streak under Brian Kelly at Notre Dame.
- On offense, the Irish scored touchdowns on all four possessions in the second half.

- Notre Dame had five scoring drives that lasted at least 10 plays and four TD drives longer than 80 yards in the game. Only one of nine Irish drives in the game did not gain over 50 yards, and only one of nine drives didn't end in Miami territory.
- The Irish rushed for 376 yards—most in a game since 2000. Of the 51 rushes, only one went for negative yardage (and Notre Dame is 22–1 since 2002 when it gains at least 200 rushing yards in a game).
- The Irish had two running backs go over 100 yards in a game for the first time since 2002, as Notre Dame rushed for 270 yards in the second half alone.
- The Irish totaled 587 yards of offense—most in a game by Notre Dame since 2005.

The Fighting Irish marching band forms the No. 125 on the Soldier Field grass during halftime to commemorate Notre Dame's 125 years of football.

- It was a dominant third quarter as 19 of 21 plays were rushes and went for 197 yards. The Irish outgained Miami 230–31 in the third quarter and outscored the 'Canes 21–0.
- Notre Dame finished the game with 34 first downs, two short of the school record.

The week off helped us, especially with Everett Golson. I thought it was the first game that he played where he exhibited some of that quick decision-making, and, in particular, right before the half we were able to lead a quick drive down the field and line up for a field goal. Though we didn't make it, we did some things there that showed that the quarterback position was coming along. On the field, he was starting to show the things that you would hope [for] after a few games into the season. We were able to run the ball well as a team, and you saw Everett run it a little more. So a little bit of all of the things that go into running the offense, we were able to see that now.

—Brian Kelly

- Miami entered the game averaging 35.6 points/game, 472.6 yards/game and 328.4 passing yards/game. But the Irish defense limited the 'Canes to three points, 201 passing yards, and 285 total yards.
- It's the first time Notre Dame has gone three straight games without allowing a TD since 1980 (that team didn't allow one for over 23 quarters).
- The Irish scoring defense now ranks second in the nation behind only Alabama.

We physically dominate a really fast football team on both sides of the ball against Miami. We were fast enough to hang with them. We physically dominate, which again was like Michigan State. We're going to change how we play. We become a physical football team. They couldn't get us off the field or run the ball at us at all.

The battle in the trenches was big against a team that has as much talent to beat any-body. We played the game the way we were going to play the game. They weren't as good at our game as we were. Everett has a great game, and we're back in business.
—*Chuck Martin*

Monday, October 8

Late Saturday night in the bowels of Soldier Field, as the Irish buses pulled out to head back to campus, Notre Dame officials received word that ESPN *College GameDay* is headed to Notre Dame this weekend. ESPN determined several weeks ago that the Notre Dame–Stanford game was under consideration. A mid-afternoon conference call today between Notre Dame and ESPN staff was followed up by a late afternoon confirmation of the set location—the Library Mall just north of Notre Dame Stadium. ESPN staff will spend all day Thursday constructing the set. The *Mike & Mike in the Morning* ESPN radio show will come live from the set from 6:00 to 10:00 AM Friday (featuring former Notre Dame football standout Mike Golic). The set will be utilized Friday for several other ESPN tapings.

"The Pit" area in front of the ESPN stage will be available for fans beginning early Saturday. The ESPNU portion of the show goes live at 9:00 AM, then *GameDay* on ESPN goes live from 10:00 AM to noon Eastern time. The staging will be cleared following the conclusion of the show, and the ESPN trucks will be loaded and on their way out by mid-to late afternoon before the game is even over.

The NBC Sports Network will work off a set in the corner of Notre Dame Stadium both Friday and Saturday. NBC plans live segments from that set during Friday night coverage of Notre Dame's hockey game from Kansas City—then will use the set throughout the day Saturday, including live postgame coverage of Notre Dame–Stanford football.

Tuesday, October 9

Notre Dame still has yet to trail in any of its football games in 2012—the only team in the country that can say that. This is the first Irish team to accomplish that through its first five games since the 1947 Notre Dame team that won a consensus national championship. So far this year in five first periods the Irish have allowed a combined single field goal. Here are more highlights:

- Notre Dame has not allowed a touchdown over its last 12 quarters (dating back to a fourth-period score by Purdue on September 8).
- Notre Dame has not allowed a touchdown in any of its last three games (against No. 10 Michigan State, No. 18 Michigan, and 4–1 Miami). The Irish have not accomplished that feat since head coach Dan Devine's final season in 1980, when the Fighting Irish defense set a school record by not allowing a touchdown in 23 straight quarters over six games.
- Notre Dame is allowing just 7.8 points per game to rank second in the nation in that category (behind Alabama's 7.0 mark). No school in the NCAA Football Bowl Subdivision has allowed fewer total touchdowns than the Irish (three).
- Notre Dame has allowed 39 combined points over its first five games in 2012. The Irish have not surrendered fewer points over their first five games of a season since 1975 when Notre Dame allowed 34.
- Notre Dame's defense has yet to allow a rushing touchdown in 2012. The Irish are one of two teams in the FBS that can still make that claim five games into the season (TCU is the other).
- The last time the Irish began a season without permitting a rushing touchdown in five straight games to start the year was 1989.

Our main objective on defense is to keep the points down. We don't know what the other side is going to bring, so we try not to worry about it. If the team can't score, then we're going to have a great chance to win. So we're interested in keeping the points down. That's everything we do. There are some core fundamentals that go along with keeping the points down that can't waver. That's where the systems are built, that's where the personnel is placed. That's where, when we make cut-ups of plays, they all have to do with point-producing moments or potential point-producing moments.

—*Bob Diaco*

Wednesday, October 10

NBC *Sports Saturday* will show an hour-long special that will provide an inside look at the Irish program. The show will feature material gained by an NFL Films crew embedded with the Irish squad during the weeks of the Michigan and Miami football games. Given the results of those two outings, Notre Dame fans figure to enjoy the show.

A couple of interesting stats pointed out by Irish coach Brian Kelly at his press conference yesterday included:

1. His Irish have won 13 of their last 15 regular-season games.
2. Notre Dame ran the ball 30 straight times Saturday against Miami.
3. The Irish have not allowed a sack on any of their last 85 pass attempts.

Notre Dame's football team will recognize Breast Cancer Awareness Month in its game against Stanford. The Irish will wear their usual home uniforms but feature pink accessories including wristbands, gloves, and socks. Notre Dame's coaching staff will wear navy hats/visors that feature pink accents. The Kelly Cares Foundation will also sell face-ka-bobs that sport coach Brian Kelly's likeness. The proceeds will support organizations, initiatives, and programs that closely align with the goals and values of the Kelly family in three pillars: health, education, and community. Specifically, the foundation focuses on breast cancer research, education and institutional advancement, and community involvement in selected initiatives and projects. The breast cancer initiative is a personal one for Brian Kelly since his wife Paqui is a two-time breast cancer survivor.

The football game Saturday between Notre Dame and Stanford will mark the first meeting between two universities ranked in the top 20 in the *U.S. News & World Report* survey "America's Best Colleges" and in the top 20 of the weekly football polls. Notre Dame is ranked No. 17 in the latest *U.S. News* survey and No. 7 in this week's football polls (AP and *USA Today*), while Stanford is No. 6 and No. 17, respectively. Stanford and Notre Dame also are at the top in the graduation rates of both the overall student bodies and student-athletes. Overall, they are tied for third among national research universities, each graduating 96 percent of their students, and among student-athletes, Notre Dame ranks first at 99 percent and Stanford is seventh at 94 percent (statistics based on the latest Graduation Success Rate figures from the NCAA).

Notre Dame ranked tied for first and Stanford ranked third among all NCAA Division I institutions in the country in combining athletic and academic achievement, according to the annual rankings released in September by the National Collegiate Scouting Association in Chicago. The NCSA Collegiate Power Rankings assess the academic and athletics standards of all NCAA and NAIA athletics programs across the country. Rankings are calculated for each college and university at the NCAA Division I, II, and III levels by averaging the academic rankings from *U.S. News & World Report*, the strength of the athletics departments by the NACDA Learfield Sports Directors' Cup ranking, plus each school's student-athlete graduation rate as provided by the NCAA.

Saturday, October 13

GameDay draws a huge crowd, thanks in part to a Brian Kelly appearance. The always-colorful Lee Corso makes it clear whom he is picking to win when he dons an entire leprechaun costume and dances a jig on stage. Irish fan Vince Vaughn (he had a supporting role in *Rudy*) makes the celebrity picks at the end of the show.

But all the pregame pageantry hardly holds a candle to the football game, a 20–13 overtime victory for Notre Dame, putting the Irish at 6–0.

Stanford had beaten Notre Dame three seasons in a row, in great part by winning the physical battles in the trenches. Brian Kelly knew his Irish team had to find a way to at least hold its own in that area to have any chance of defeating the 17th-ranked Cardinal in 2012.

Seventh-rated and unbeaten Notre Dame couldn't have made its point in that regard any more emphatically than with a clutch goal-line stand that enabled the Irish to stop Stanford just short of the end zone in a 20–13 overtime victory in the rain at Notre Dame Stadium.

A full house of 80,795 fans viewed the drama at Notre Dame Stadium in a game televised by NBC. The victory moved Notre Dame to 6–0.

After the Irish came back from a first-half touchdown deficit to tie the game on a field goal with 20 seconds remaining in regulation, Notre Dame took the lead on a seven-yard scoring pass from reserve quarterback Tommy Rees to TJ Jones—with Jones reaching behind his body to snag the throw just inside the goal line.

Rees came on late after starter Everett Golson took a helmet to the head—and Rees ended up leading both the end of the late field-goal drive and the overtime possession (he completed all four of his passes for 43 yards). Maybe the biggest throw came on third-and-eight in the overtime when he found Theo Riddick for 16 yards.

Stanford came right back on its overtime possession to achieve a first down at the Irish 4 as the rain came down. Cardinal back Stepfan Taylor, who ended up with 102 rushing yards, carried on the first three downs for one yard, two yards, and maybe a foot on third down. On fourth down Taylor tried the middle again, only to be turned back by Notre Dame's Carlo Calabrese and his teammates. Taylor tried to reach the ball past the goal line, but officials blew the whistle, and the Notre Dame celebration was on. A booth review confirmed the Irish win.

It doesn't matter if the ball is on the goal line, their 1-yard line, or our 1-yard line—we're going to play the same. That's the mentality we have, and that growth has shown this year and will continue to get better.

—*Manti Te'o*

The Irish ground out 150 rushing yards in the victory—66 for Cierre Wood, 45 for Riddick, and 41 for Golson. Golson was true on 12 of his 24 throws for 141 yards before his injury. Tyler Eifert (four catches for 57 yards) and Jones (four for 52) paced the Irish receivers.

Linebacker Manti Te'o headed up the Notre Dame tackling corps with 11, while Zeke Motta added nine and Matthias Farley eight.

Both teams struggled to muster much on offense early against stout defenses. Golson lost a fumble on Notre Dame's first possession, and Stanford's Josh Nunes saw the second Cardinal drive come to a screeching halt when Bennett Jackson intercepted a pass at the Irish 1.

Nunes threw a second first-period interception, which Farley returned 49 yards to the Stanford 16. Four plays later Kyle Brindza put the Irish on the board with a 29-yard field goal at 0:36 of the opening period.

Former Irish football standout—and father of current player Mike Golic Jr.—Mike Golic interviews head coach Brian Kelly on ESPN's GameDay *prior to the game vs. Stanford.*

Stanford drove to the Irish 8 in the second period, only to have its 25-yard field-goal attempt blocked by Stephon Tuitt. Then, with the Irish backed up in the shadow of their goal posts, Golson was sacked in his own end zone and lost the football—and Stanford's Chase Thomas recovered for a Cardinal TD at the 6:06 to go in the half.

After the Irish couldn't convert anything into points after reaching the Stanford 10, the Cardinal marched to the Notre Dame 30, and Jordan Williamson's 48-yard field goal made it 10–3 Stanford as the first half ended.

Neither team scored in the third period, with Notre Dame's best chance thwarted when Golson fumbled the ball away at the Stanford 17 after a 20-yard rushing gain.

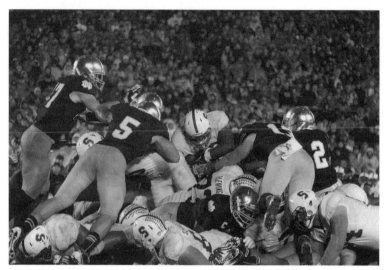

The Notre Dame defense's clutch goal-line stand against Stanford in overtime clinched the 20–13 win for the Irish.

After a Stanford punt late in the third period, the Irish began at their own 48. Golson hit Riddick for 23 yards, then from the Stanford 24 found Eifert for the tying TD 45 seconds into the final period.

Stanford came right back with a 16-play, 68-yard possession—that featured three critical third-down conversions—with Williamson's 27-yard field goal at the 6:12 mark, making it 13–10 for the Cardinal.

Notre Dame answered with a 12-play, 79-yard drive of its own. Golson started the possession but left the game after his four-yard gain ended on a helmet-to-helmet hit (and personal foul) to reach the Stanford 34. Rees came on, completed his only pass attempt to Eifert, and then saw the Irish benefit from a third-down pass-interference penalty against the Cardinal.

After the Irish reached the Stanford 5, Brindza converted a 22-yard field goal with 20 seconds remaining in regulation to send the game to overtime.

For the Stanford game we talked about bringing the same kind of mentality that we had at Michigan State, because this was going to be a similar kind of game. There were going to be two very good defenses. It was going to be about trying to find a way offensively to get points on the board. It wasn't pretty, but it was certainly one of those games where you were fighting for every yard.

We talked about how we have to fight for every inch of this game, and as it turned out with the goal-line stand at the end, it was certainly apropos because we did fight for inches.

I was able to get in front of the team, and I was able to tell them that what they accomplished was real. But the margin for error is so slim with this group that the way we played the game, we cannot go into any game without playing our very best. We're capable of losing to anybody, and we're capable of beating anybody. So those messages were heard each and every week because of the way the games were played.

—Brian Kelly

Monday, October 15

Stanford–Notre Dame (5.2 million) was the most-watched Notre Dame afternoon game on NBC in more than two years (Michigan, 7 million, September 11, 2010)—and it was the most-watched Notre Dame game on NBC featuring a team other than Michigan or USC in more than six years, since Penn State on September 9, 2006 (6.9 million).

Stanford was a little bit different. That was the ultimate physical test. This is the team that knows how they want to play—physical and toe-to-toe, which is what we did against Miami, against Michigan State. And that's what coach [Kelly] said. We had talked about being physical all year—kind of the style of the past. If you can hang with Stanford in that aspect, that means something, because we hadn't the first two years.

As we looked at the schedule, the question is, are we going to beat Stanford? They continually punch us in the mouth, and we've got to counter-punch. We have to change this.

Obviously, we went toe to toe, and offensively we ran for 150, 160 yards against a team where in the past we couldn't run against them at all. Defensively we went the whole game, then the goal-line stand again. Tommy came in again and did what Tommy did after Everett was dinged. So it worked out.

—*Chuck Martin*

Tuesday, October 16

Jim Rome's interview show this week features a chat with Manti Te'o. CBSSports.com picked a Midseason College Football All-America team and had Te'o on the first team and Tyler Eifert and Stephon Tuitt on the second team. SI.com did the same and had Te'o on the first team and Tuitt on the second.

Friday, October 19

British golfer and TV commentator Nick Faldo is in town for the Notre Dame–BYU football game. He traded Irish head coach Brian Kelly a copy of his new book *A Swing for Life* for a box of Kelly-autographed golf balls in a post–pep rally visit Friday night.

Saturday, October 20

The Irish put their unbeaten record and No. 5 ranking on the line at Notre Dame Stadium against fellow independent BYU.

Notre Dame ran for 270 ground yards against the third-ranked rushing defense in the country as the Irish came from behind at Notre Dame Stadium to stave off BYU 17–14.

With 80,795 fans viewing the game in person, NBC televised the Irish advancing their record to 7–0.

With regular quarterback Everett Golson sidelined after a hit to the head a week earlier in the win over Stanford, junior Tommy Rees earned the call and for the most part let his offensive line and backs carry the day. Rees completed six of his first seven throws for 86 yards and a

Backup quarterback Tommy Rees started against BYU in place of the injured Everett Golson and led the Irish to a 17–14 win. Photo courtesy of AP Images

Tight end Tyler Eifert makes a grab during Notre Dame's win vs. BYU.

touchdown in the opening period—then the Irish attempted only three passes the entire second half.

Senior Theo Riddick paced the ground attack with a career-high 143 yards on 15 attempts, while Cierre Wood added another 114 yards on 18 carries.

The Cougars had only 66 rushing yards of their own, with quarterback Riley Nelson connecting on 23 of his 36 throws for 177 yards, two touchdowns, and two interceptions.

The Irish missed a 40-yard field goal on their initial offensive possession, and linebacker Manti Te'o picked off a Nelson throw to stop the first BYU attempt.

Notre Dame got on the board first, driving 64 yards late in the first period. Rees found tight end Tyler Eifert for 29 yards to open the drive, then Wood carried for 22 yards to the BYU 13. Rees put the points on the board with a four-yard throw to Eifert, and it began 7–0 for Notre Dame with 1:30 remaining in the opening period.

The Irish missed another field goal and threw an interception in the second period—and BYU responded with a pair of TD drives and Nelson scoring passes. After an Irish punt, the Cougars traveled 56 yards in eight plays, with Nelson connecting with Cody Hoffman for six yards to tie the contest at seven. That ended a Notre Dame defensive streak of 17 straight periods without allowing an opponent an offensive TD.

After a Kyle Van Noy interception three plays into an Irish possession, BYU started at the Notre Dame 30 and needed four plays to take the lead. A Nelson throw to Kaneakua Friel from two yards out made it a 14–7 Irish halftime deficit.

After a missed BYU field goal from 46 yards, Notre Dame came back with a three-pointer of its own. Kyle Brindza hit from 24 yards away to cut the BYU lead to 14–10 with 2:25 left in the third period. Riddick's career-long 55-yard run keyed that 65-yard Irish possession.

After a three-and-out by BYU, Notre Dame took over at 1:26 of the third period and drove for what proved to be the winning and final points of the game. The possession began with a first-down throw for 32 yards from Rees to TJ Jones to the BYU 41, Notre Dame's lone second-half pass completion. Riddick ran 19 yards to the Cougars 5, then on third-and-goal George Atkinson III found the end zone from the 2 for a 17–14 Notre Dame advantage with 12:52 left in the game.

BYU drove from its own 16 to the Irish 34 in 13 plays, but Nelson misfired on a third-and-13 pass attempt, and the visitors were forced to punt. Notre Dame moved from its own 20 to the BYU 32 before a Ben Turk punt into the end zone. The Cougars' last-gasp attempt ended when Danny Spond intercepted Nelson's first-down throw at the BYU 39.

Notre Dame finished with 157 second-half running yards on 24 attempts. Te'o again paced the Irish defense with 10 stops and an interception, while KeiVarae Russell, Matthias Farley, and Prince Shembo each had six tackles. The Notre Dame defense put up seven tackles for losses and four sacks. Here are some leftover notes from Notre Dame's 17–14 win over BYU:

- Notre Dame is now 7–1 in its last eight games decided by seven points or less (after going 2–9 in the previous 11 in that category).
- In the second half, Notre Dame averaged 7.0 yards per play, compared to 3.7 for BYU.
- Notre Dame rushed for 270 yards against the third-rated rushing defense in the country, which had been allowing 67.9 rushing yards per game.
- Notre Dame's 270 rushing yards were the most against BYU in the last 16 Cougars games and second most in last 30 BYU games.
- The Irish averaged 6.3 yards per rush against a defense that had been allowing 2.2 yards per rush.
- Over its last three games, Notre Dame has combined to rush for 796 yards (138 attempts) for 5.8 yards per carry and six rushing TDs.
- Notre Dame has rushed for more yards in its last three games combined than 15 FBS teams have in their entire seasons.
- Five of Notre Dame's wins this season have come with the Irish scoring between 13 and 20 points.

Irish middle linebacker Manti Te'o in action against BYU.

A lot of people talked about the BYU game. That was a quality opponent that a lot of people didn't take seriously, and that's one of the things at Notre Dame that you've got to fight. People look at the schedule and go, "Oh, that's BYU." Well, that was a really good football team. They're a lot like a Navy, an Army, or an Air Force, where they do some exotic things especially on defense. With only a few days to prepare, that makes it hard for you. Again, very good defense on our part. They weren't able to run the football, and offensively we did enough and controlled the flow of the game.

—*Brian Kelly*

Now Everett is still dinged, so we go into the BYU game with a new starter. It's back-to-back home games after the Stanford win, and we aren't very pretty for three quarters, but we find a way to come out smelling like a rose.

—*Chuck Martin*

Sunday, October 21

Notre Dame's visit to Oklahoma this weekend brings back some comparisons to a somewhat similar matchup just a decade ago when an unbeaten Irish team traveled to Florida State:

2002	2012
Notre Dame's record: 7–0	Notre Dame's record: 7–0
Notre Dame's rank: No. 6 (AP)	Notre Dame's rank: No. 5 (AP)
Florida State's record: 5–2	Oklahoma's record: 5–1
Florida State's rank: No. 11 (AP)	Oklahoma's rank: No. 8 (AP)
Notre Dame's first-ever visit to Tallahassee	Notre Dame is making its first visit to Norman since 1966
Notre Dame's rank in total defense: No. 10 (275.86 yards/game)	Notre Dame's rank in total defense: No. 6 (280.71 yards/game)
Notre Dame's rank in scoring defense: No. 3 (12.0 points/game)	Notre Dame's rank in scoring defense: No. 2 (9.43 points/game)
Notre Dame's rank in pass efficiency defense: No. 8	Notre Dame's rank in pass efficiency defense: No. 8
Notre Dame's rank in rushing defense: No. 6 (80.14 yards/game)	Notre Dame's rank in rushing defense: No. 15 (106.71 yards/game)
Notre Dame's rank in turnover margin: No. 17 (plus-8)	Notre Dame's rank in turnover margin: No. 11 (plus-9)
Rushing TDs allowed by Notre Dame: 3	Rushing TDs allowed by Notre Dame: 0
Florida State's rank in scoring: No. 12 (36.86 points/game)	Oklahoma's rank in scoring: No. 5 (44.67 points/game)
Irish fans harkened back to a win over Florida State in 1993 when the Seminoles were No. 1.	Irish fans harkened back to a win over Oklahoma in 1957 when the Sooners were No. 1 and had won 47 straight.

Here are some of coach Brian Kelly's comments from his afternoon media teleconference:

- "I think [the players] know they haven't arrived. And even being fifth in the country and 7–0—you can say that, that they haven't arrived, that they haven't reached the level that they can. And yet I think it is a very good place to be. There's a lot of things that we know we can improve on. If you're 7–0 and fifth in the country and you think you've arrived, then that's where as a coach and a team, you're in peril."

- "With Oklahoma, it's the balance on offense. It's not just Landry Jones. If it's just Landry Jones, then they're not where they are. It's their ability to run the football equally as well as throwing the football. It's one of the most balanced offenses in the country in terms of—they can play physical, they can throw the ball, and, of course, Landry Jones has got those weapons that allow him to be so successful. The offense is certainly about Landry Jones, but more importantly, it's the balance that they have."

- "With Everett Golson, I think it's bits and pieces throughout the entire year, at Michigan State in a very hostile environment, and then in big-game situations where we're playing on the road in Chicago. It's just a cumulative effect. In other words, all the pieces that come together for him to make him a better quarterback than he was earlier in the year is his experience, and we think he'll build on that and should not have any problem playing in a big environment at Oklahoma because he's already done it. If you have a running game behind you that you can rely on when things get tough, I think all quarterbacks love that opportunity. It makes it easier for them to be more successful throwing the football. I think the big key for him is he knows going in that he doesn't have to do it himself. He can rely on others and especially guys like [Tyler] Eifert and TJ Jones and a veteran offensive line and the backs that we saw run the last couple of weeks."

- "I don't know if I would characterize it as what went wrong [against BYU]. When we look at—let's just take an offensive standpoint. Two missed field goals, those conversions, those have to be touchdowns on those drives. We can't settle for field goals. I look at it and make assessments as to what we did on those drives. We had a snap infraction that put us in a third-and-nine situation, and then we come back and miss the field goal. Then we come back again with a great drive and a big run and we can't convert a couple of runs. As we go through it, what we're looking for is how we can put more points on the board. Settling for field goals has really been my focus—we left too many points out there. We've got to put more points on the board."

- "Our preparation this week? It'll be the same. You have to play better and continue to improve during the week. It only counts as one. So we'll do the things that we've done leading up to it. We won't change anything in our approach. But our players understand that they've got to go on the road against a top 10 team and have to play extremely well. We've done this already. We went on the road against a top 10 team in Michigan State and beat them. We're going to have to do the same thing here."

- "I think probably the Purdue game and then going on the road against Michigan State probably instilled the most confidence in our group. I'd probably single out those two games where they were both close, competitive games, and then of course Michigan at 13–6. Those games, when you win those close games early in the season, it kind of sets it for the rest of the year."

- "I thought that the first half [vs. BYU] wasn't our best half, but our second half was, and it's about a four-quarter game. No, I don't look for margin of score. I just want our guys to compete and prepare well. If they prepare well and compete on Saturdays, we'll win enough games. I really don't care how many we win them by."

- "If you take back-to-back weeks and look at what we did in the second half in running the football [vs. BYU], it's a real positive for us. We've got to do some other things a little bit more efficiently, but if you take the last two weeks and take the defense that we have, continue to be solid in the special teams, and know that you can run the football against two really good defenses, that's a pretty good feeling at the end of the day, and I think we carry that moving forward against Oklahoma."
- "People talk about being flat. I thought our guys had very good intensity [vs. BYU], very consistent in their approach, in their preparation. We were sloppy. We had some sloppy play in terms of we threw an interception, we had a personal foul. It was more about some sloppiness than it was intensity. I was pleased with the way we came out, other than those errors I mentioned."

The Irish came from behind to erase halftime deficits in each of the last two football games against Stanford and BYU:

- Stanford (trailed 10–3 at half, won 20–13 in OT)
- BYU (trailed 14–7 at half, won 17–14)

The last time Notre Dame won two straight games by coming from behind at the half was more than 40 years ago—in the final game of the 1978 campaign and the opener of 1979:

- Houston in 1979 Cotton Bowl (trailed 20–12 at half, won 35–34)
- at Michigan (trailed 10–6 at half, won 12–10)

When was the last time you can remember a scenario that featured Notre Dame winning football games with two different quarterbacks starting and playing in different weeks?

ESPN's *College GameDay* program heads to Norman this weekend for Notre Dame–Oklahoma. That makes two appearances at Irish games in a three-week span. Previous seasons in which *GameDay* has covered Irish games twice include 1999 (Michigan and Tennessee), 2002 (Air Force and Florida State), 2005 (Pittsburgh and USC), and 2006 (Georgia Tech and USC).

Tuesday, October 23

Notre Dame is currently averaging 193.9 rushing yards per game. If that figure held up the rest of the way, it would represent Notre Dame's best in that category since a 213.4 mark in 2000.

The Irish have won four games this year by seven points or less. Most recently, the 2009 Notre Dame team also had four and the 2002 team had five. The record is six in 1939.

Oklahoma coach Bob Stoops has a 79–4 record at home since he began in Norman in 1999. The only teams to beat a Stoops-coached Sooners team in Norman are Kansas State in 2012, Texas Tech in 2011, TCU in 2005, and Oklahoma State in 2001.

Of Notre Dame's eight turnovers this season, seven have happened at Notre Dame Stadium and only one (an interception against Navy in Dublin) has happened on the road. The Irish did not have a turnover in away or neutral site games against Michigan State and Miami (Chicago).

Notre Dame senior linebacker Manti Te'o was named a Butkus Award semifinalist and Lott Trophy quarterfinalist today. Te'o is one of four players in the nation to be recognized on each list.

Te'o also has been selected a 2012 National Scholar-Athlete by the National Football Foundation. As a National Scholar-Athlete, Te'o receives an $18,000 postgraduate scholarship. Fifteen class members were selected this year from a nationwide pool of 147 semifinalists. Te'o is the 17th Notre Dame football player to receive the scholarship and the third in the last six years (John Carlson, 2007; Chris Stewart, 2010). Only Nebraska (20) and Ohio State (19) have had more players selected since the program began in 1959. Set to graduate this December with a degree in graphic design, the Laie, Hawaii, native owns a 3.32 cumulative grade-point average and was named the 2011 Notre Dame Football Student-Athlete of the Year. He was also selected as a second-team Academic All-America honoree as a junior.

So Te'o will be one of the honored guests at the National Football Foundation's Annual Awards Dinner on Tuesday, December 4, in New York City. Also honored at the awards dinner will be former Notre Dame tight end and 2012 College Football Hall of Fame inductee Dave Casper.

Thursday, October 25

Fox Sports today published a feature by Greg Couch about Irish line-backer Manti Te'o that told volumes about the Notre Dame linebacker. Here are excerpts:

> Manti Te'o didn't even know Bridget Smith. They were two people from two worlds: A Mormon football star at Notre Dame who is a Hawaiian of Samoan descent. A dying 12-year-old Catholic girl from suburban Detroit.
>
> "Dear Mr. and Mrs. Smith." Te'o wrote an emotional letter, via email. Picture a big, tough linebacker sitting at his

computer, "definitely crying," as he said, over someone else's pain, some stranger's pain.

All he had known about Bridget, all he had been told through a mutual friend, was that Bridget's brain tumor was finally proving too powerful and that she wasn't going to get out of the hospital again. And she loved Notre Dame football and Manti Te'o.

"My whole thing was just to reach out and let them know I'm here. I wrote her parents," Te'o said in a private moment the other day.

"Just letting them know that the heavenly father is always there. Although it may not seem like it right now, He's always there to help. It was definitely hard to write."

On the other end of that email were Brian and Louise Smith. Brian, a Notre Dame alum and fan, and Louise, a St. Mary's alum. They had watched the Notre Dame–Michigan game with Bridget just a few weeks earlier in the University of Michigan Intensive Care Unit. On Friday, October 5, they were planning to disconnect Bridget's ventilator at 3:00 PM.

It would be her last day.

That morning, they casually opened their email and saw one that had come from: MANTI TE'O. He would pour out his feelings and connect with the Smiths' world.

"We opened that letter that morning, and it was just a bright spot on the saddest day of our lives," Louise Smith said. "We read it to her; we shared with her what it said. They say hearing is the last thing to go. I don't know. I believe she internalized it.

"It's so encouraging to have someone in that position know there's something more important than football, more important than athletics."

Friday, October 26

Former Oklahoma coach Barry Switzer stopped by the Sooners' Memorial Stadium and visited with Irish coach Brian Kelly briefly this afternoon. The Irish team flew into Oklahoma City and drove to Norman and spent close to a half-hour at the stadium, with ESPN's *GameDay* set just outside the Sooners' home facility.

Saturday, October 27

It's no easy drive to arrive at Memorial Stadium in Norman, with traffic and fans packing the narrow roadways in the vicinity of the stadium. It's an impressive atmosphere in prime time as the Sooners and Irish prepare to do battle.

Unbeaten Notre Dame stated its best case yet for earning a tag as a legitimate national championship contender—as the fifth-ranked Irish ran off 17 straight fourth-quarter points to dispatch eighth-rated Oklahoma at Memorial Stadium in Norman, Oklahoma, in a prime-time outing televised by ABC.

After the two teams battled to a 13–13 deadlock following a Sooners touchdown with a little more than nine minutes remaining in the game, the Irish responded in definitive fashion.

First, quarterback Everett Golson made maybe the biggest play of the night, hitting seldom-used freshman receiver Chris Brown for a 50-yard pass play (his first career reception) on a second down from the Irish 35. That set Golson and his teammates up at the Oklahoma 15, and five plays later the Notre Dame signal-caller ran it in from the 1 for a 20–13 Irish lead at the 5:05 mark as the visitors went ahead for good.

Next, senior linebacker Manti Te'o ended the Sooners response with a diving interception of a pass (off the hands of Jalen Saunders after a Dan Fox hit) that was reviewed by officials and ultimately resulted in an Irish first down at the Sooners 45. The Irish ran four plays and reached the Oklahoma 29, where Kyle Brindza connected on a 46-yard field goal to make it 23–13 with 3:22 remaining.

Finally, after Oklahoma lost the ball on downs, the Irish drove 20 yards for the final points, with Theo Riddick running 15 yards to push the Irish lead to 30–13 with only 1:36 left.

Oklahoma quarterback Landry Jones finished with 356 passing yards, but Notre Dame's defense allowed only 15 net rushing yards to the home-standing Sooners who had lost only four previous home games (against 79 wins) during the Bob Stoops era. The win moved the Irish to 8–0.

Meanwhile, a balanced Irish attack included 215 rushing yards—74 each by Riddick and Cierre Wood, with both scoring a touchdown. Sixty-two of Wood's yards came on an electric first-period TD dash that gave Notre Dame a 7–3 advantage at the end of the opening quarter.

Golson threw for 177 yards and ran for another 64.

Te'o made the most noise for the Irish defense, finishing with a game-high 11 tackles (all in the first half) to go with his fifth interception, two tackles for loss, and one attention-grabbing sack of Jones on a third down early in the second period.

The Sooners marched 71 yards on their second possession, ending in a 28-yard Mike Hunnicutt field goal after stalling at the Notre Dame 11. Wood's 62-yard TD run came on the second play of the ensuing Irish possession.

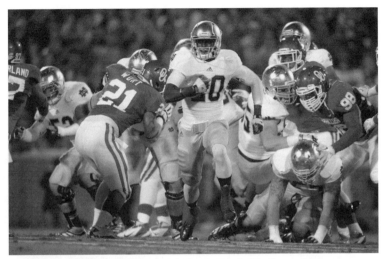

Irish running back Cierre Wood breaks into the open against the Sooners' defense.

Midway through the second period, Notre Dame drove 64 yards from its own 19, with Golson twice connecting on key third-down throws—once to DaVaris Daniels and once to Robby Toma. From the Oklahoma 17 Kyle Brindza kicked a 34-yard field goal to make it 10–3 for the Irish.

Oklahoma answered with a 66-yard drive of its own, with Hunnicutt nailing a 30-yard field goal in the final minute of the opening half for a 10–6 Irish halftime lead. The Sooners managed only three net rushing yards in the first 30 minutes, despite running 18 more plays than Notre Dame.

Neither team scored in the third period, with Brindza misfiring on a 35-yard field-goal attempt at the 8:06 mark. Notre Dame drove from its own 3 to the Oklahoma 27, where Brindza found the mark from 44 yards out five plays into the final period for a 13–6 advantage.

Oklahoma's only TD of the night came on a 52-yard drive, with backup quarterback Blake Bell scoring from the 1. Jones' 35-yard completion to Saunders marked the biggest play of that march. That tied it at 13 before the Irish dominated the rest of the contest.

Saunders finished with 15 catches for 181 yards. TJ Jones had five receptions for 55 yards for the Irish. Against the Sooners aerial attack, Irish cornerbacks KeiVarae Russell and Bennett Jackson were outstanding, making nine and eight tackles, respectively.

Notre Dame dominated time of possession in the second half—holding the ball for 19:57 in the final two periods compared to 10:03 for Oklahoma. The Irish scored 20 fourth-period points, and their

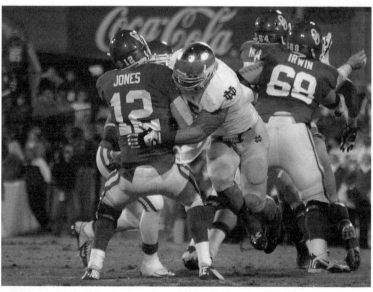

Oklahoma quarterback Landry Jones is taken down by Notre Dame's Manti Te'o for a drive-ending sack early in the second quarter.

defense limited a Sooners squad averaging over 44 points per game to less than 14.

The victory marked Notre Dame's second on the road over a team ranked in the top 10 and its fourth against a ranked opponent (most in the nation)—with a stadium-record crowd of 86,031 watching.

Here are leftover notes from Notre Dame's 30–13 victory over Oklahoma:

- Notre Dame converted seven of its last 12 third-down attempts.
- The Irish now have played two top 10–rated opponents on the road and not committed a turnover in either game (the Irish are 9–0 under Brian Kelly when playing turnover-free football).
- It's the first time Notre Dame has posted two road wins over top 10 teams since 1966 (that year, No. 10 Oklahoma and No. 10 USC).
- Cierre Wood and Theo Riddick Saturday combined to rush 26 times for 158 yards and average 6.21 yards per carry.
- The 13 points by Oklahoma marked the second-fewest ever scored by Oklahoma at home during the Bob Stoops era (begun in 1999).
- The 15 net rushing yards by Oklahoma marked its fewest in a game since 2009 and the seventh fewest in Oklahoma history.
- Manti Te'o's five interceptions tie the Notre Dame record for most interceptions in a season by a linebacker (with John Pergine in 1966 and Lyron Cobbins in 1995).

Going to Oklahoma, one thing with this group at that time that we had a feel for was that they liked playing on the road at night and in kind of an electric environment. When we came out in that stadium, it was electric. Our guys really enjoyed that atmosphere. They relished the opportunity to play in those circumstances.

I didn't know if we were going to win or lose the game, but I told our staff our guys are not intimidated by the environment. As a matter of fact, they were really comfortable in it. Once we were able to stop them early on, I think there was a lot of confidence that was being gained throughout the entire sideline. Certainly getting on the board first helped in that as well.

—Brian Kelly

We've got Oklahoma, and you know you have to stop the run. You have to get after the pass, which we did. They had a bunch of completions, but we said, offensively we're going to slow this game down. If it goes well, we're trying to get it to the fourth quarter and take it then. So our whole game plan for three quarters offensively was to chase time off the clock. We hit a big one early. But the third quarter was the best. We had two long drives in the third quarter and six points.

At our Thursday meeting that week we talked about the plan. Then the players started believing. We told them how we could win, and there was still some doubt. Some kids had been here through some rough times, and they're wondering, *Can we really guard them?* And not only did we do it, we told them exactly how we were going to do it.

I think this is when Everett realized our commitment to him, because he was the starter going to Norman even though Tommy had played the whole game the week before against BYU and had finished strong against Stanford. Everett understands now he's our guy.

It's a lot like Michigan State, but even better. The game went the same way, we pull away and win by 17. Do all the things right in the fourth quarter. They tie in the fourth quarter, and we score 17 straight, and defense does it with big interceptions and big stops, and offense with Chris Brown.

The biggest catch all season is by Chris Brown. Talk about writing a story. Once again, Disney makes it, but they don't believe it. No way that guy's first catch is going to be Week 8 in Norman. And it's in the fourth quarter, not the first quarter. It's a 55-yard bomb, and it's the one thing you still scratch your head about. But, again, coach [Kelly] using all his resources, we're always ready, always right place, right time. He [Brown] probably played five snaps the whole game. Plus, we think we're past any quarterback issues at all because Everett plays great at Oklahoma running and throwing.

—Chuck Martin

Lost in the Notre Dame football win at Oklahoma were the 15 receptions (for 181 yards) by Sooners wide receiver Jalen Saunders. That's the most catches ever in a single game against Notre Dame. The previous high was 14 by three players—Jim Price of Stanford in 1989, John Jackson of USC in 1989, and Robert Lavette of Georgia Tech in 1981.

The attendance at the Notre Dame–Oklahoma football game in Norman of 86,031 marked the largest crowd ever to see a sporting event in the state of Oklahoma.

We never really had this crescendo moment where we sat down and thought something had happened that told us we would be successful this year. We set up the business of the day every day so we don't even have time to look at and think about those things. We're just interested in having the very best defense we can possibly have that particular day, and when you focus that kind of energy and that kind of intense, drilled-down focus on a job, we really don't spend a lot of time thinking about anything else.

—Bob Diaco

There were plenty of defensive heroes for Notre Dame in the football win at Oklahoma—and none bigger than Manti Te'o with his 11 first-half tackles plus a sack and interception. But don't overlook the tackling of the Irish corners—true freshman KeiVarae Russell made nine tackles (six solo), and Bennett Jackson made eight (seven solo). Neither player had started a game at the college level until this season.

Every week during the year it's about where can our next opponent hurt us? Where do their strengths match up? Okay, we can't let them do this. They may beat us and be good enough to beat us. Offensively, how can we manage this to give ourselves a chance? And every week we did a very good job of not allowing the team to do things we didn't want it to do.

We didn't always do all the things we wanted to do at the level we wanted to do them. But we also look back at the way we played the game—how we thought we could win. And Oklahoma is the best example of that.

Exactly what we said on Thursday going into the Oklahoma game we executed on Saturday. There were things we worried about that hurt us in that game, but it didn't cost us the game. If we felt like we were mismatched here, we'll protect it, and rely on our strengths. And everything we said on that Thursday meeting is exactly how the game played out. If you sat in the Thursday meeting and watched the Saturday game, it would be, okay, they said A, B, C, and D needs to happen for Notre Dame to win on the road at Oklahoma as a 13-point underdog. Well, A, B, C, and D happened and probably better than we hoped. And the team believes even more.

—*Chuck Martin*

Monday, October 29

Notre Dame's No. 3 Bowl Championship Series ranking this week ties its best ever in the BCS poll (from the 2002 season). This marks the first time the Irish have been ranked in the top five in the BCS poll in three straight weeks. The Irish are tied with Kansas State for first in the computer rankings, with the Irish rating No. 1 in two of the computer polls (Colley Matrix and Massey) and No. 2 in the other four. In 2002 the Irish ranked third in the first two BCS polls of the season before dropping after a loss to Boston College.

How rare is an 8–0 start for Notre Dame in football? It's happened 20 times (including 2012). If the Irish can win this weekend, it would be the 16th time they've started 9–0.

Notre Dame's Zeke Motta today was named one of 15 semifinalists for the Jim Thorpe Award that goes to the best defensive back in the country. Three finalists will be named November 19.

When Pittsburgh heads to Notre Dame Stadium Saturday, it will mark the 12th time the Panthers have faced an Irish team ranked fourth nationally (AP poll) or better. The only Pitt win in those meetings came in 1987, a 30–22 victory at Pitt Stadium over the fourth-rated Irish.

Pittsburgh owns five other wins over ranked Notre Dame football teams among its 20 series victories over the Irish—and all five were played at Notre Dame Stadium:

- 1937: 21–6 over No. 12 Notre Dame (Pitt was ranked No. 3)
- 1952: 22–9 over No. 8 Notre Dame
- 1976: 31–10 over No. 11 Notre Dame (Pitt was ranked No. 9)
- 1983: 21–16 over No. 18 Notre Dame
- 2004: 41–38 over No. 24 Notre Dame

Tuesday, October 30

Here's what the various Heisman Trophy analysts say this week about Notre Dame's Manti Te'o:

- SI.com (Zac Ellis) lists Te'o second this week behind Kansas State's Collin Klein. In the poll of SI staffers, Klein got all but one of nine first-place votes, while Te'o was listed among the top three on all nine ballots.

- *Sporting News* puts Te'o third behind Klein and Ohio State's Braxton Miller.
- ESPN's poll of experts has Te'o second behind Klein—with Te'o receiving six second-place votes (to four for Oregon's Kenjon Banner).
- The CBSSports.com Heisman Straw Poll (votes from 11 media members on a 3-2-1 basis) has Klein first this week (31 points, 10 first-place votes), Te'o second (13 points), and USC receiver Marqise Lee third (seven points).

Any doubts about Notre Dame's place among the nation's top 10 teams were put to rest when the Fighting Irish (8–0) won a 30–13 blockbuster at No. 8 Oklahoma to earn Tostitos Fiesta Bowl National Team of the Week honors for games of the weekend of October 27. A banner noting the Fiesta Bowl honor hung on the wall on the landing of a stairwell in the Guglielmino Athletic Complex long after the season ended.

The Notre Dame–Oklahoma football game Saturday night on ABC Sports received a final 5.2 rating.

Chapter 7

November

Saturday, November 3

Another Saturday, another Irish football victory. This one had to qualify as the most unlikely to date.

Fourth-rated Notre Dame kept its unbeaten streak alive with a two-touchdown final-period comeback in regulation, then needed three overtime periods before holding off a game Pittsburgh team 29–26 in Notre Dame Stadium.

NBC televised the action, while 80,795 fans jammed Notre Dame's home stadium.

Fortune nearly turned against the Irish in the second overtime when running back Cierre Wood appeared to be heading for the go-ahead touchdown, only to fumble the ball into the end zone in midair just short of the goal line. Needing only a field goal to win, the Panthers' Kevin Harper couldn't connect from 33 yards away, pushing the try to the right.

Harper came back to open the third overtime with a 44-yard field goal to temporarily give his team the lead. Notre Dame quarterback

Irish quarterback Everett Golson (5) confers with head coach Brian Kelly during a break in play during Notre Dame's nail-biting 29–26 triple-overtime victory over Pittsburgh.

Everett Golson, who started the game but gave way for a while to Tommy Rees, threw to Theo Riddick for 11 yards on second down, then converted a third-and-three opportunity with a six-yard run of his own. His quarterback sneak from the 1 won the game for the Irish and moved his team to 9–0.

With his team down 20–6 entering the final quarter, Golson capped off a 71-yard drive with an 11-yard scoring play to TJ Jones, only to see Kyle Brindza miss the PAT for a 20–12 margin.

The Irish next drove to the Panthers 7, only to see the 91-yard, 15-play drive end when Golson threw an interception in the end zone with 3:39 left in regulation. After the Irish defense forced a three-and-out by Pitt, Notre Dame took over at midfield with 3:03 remaining—and Golson on first down connected with DaVaris Daniels for 45 yards. Golson and Riddick hooked up for a five-yard TD on the next play, and after Golson ran in the two-point conversion, the game became tied at 20 at the 2:11 mark.

Golson threw for 94 yards in the final period, and the Irish added another 74 on the ground in the last 15 minutes to pull off the two-TD comeback. That set the stage for the overtime dramatics.

Golson finished 23-of-42 passing for 227 yards and rushed for another 74 on 15 carries. Rees entered the game late in the second period when the Irish went without a first-half TD, but Golson came back midway through the third period after Rees threw an interception that turned into a Pittsburgh TD and a 17–6 Panthers advantage.

The Irish ended up with a huge, 522–308 advantage in total yards, including a 34–13 edge in first downs. Notre Dame converted 10 of 20 third downs, compared to one of 14 for Pitt. The Irish ran 104 plays to 62 for Pittsburgh and controlled the ball for almost 11 more minutes than the Panthers.

Ray Graham did most of the Panthers damage himself, rushing for 172 yards and scoring the only first-half TD by either team on a 16-yard run. He became the first opposing running back to score a rushing TD versus the Irish in 2012.

Riddick ran for 85 yards, while Daniels made seven catches for 86 yards, Tyler Eifert had six for 62, Robby Toma six for 50, and Jones five for 53.

The Irish began the game impressively, driving 60 and 89 yards on their first two possessions to produce a pair of Brindza field goals. The initial drive lasted a workmanlike 14 plays, and the second featured 18 and ended on the Pitt 2. In between, the Panthers added a field goal of their own, set up by a 55-yard Graham run.

After those two field goals, Notre Dame's offense sputtered—with six straight possessions producing four punts, a missed field goal, and an interception. Meanwhile, Graham's TD run at 3:55 of the second period made it 10–6 for the Panthers. Tino Suseri's nine-yard scoring pass to J.P. Holtz after the Rees interception pushed the lead to 17–6 and a 48-yard Graham rush put the Panthers in position for a 21-yard Harper three-pointer at the 0:58 mark for a 20–6 advantage.

Both teams scored three points in the first overtime. Pitt got as far as the Irish 19 before a false-start penalty eventually led to a 41-yard Harper field goal. Notre Dame couldn't negotiate a first down, so Brindza connected from 37 yards, and the first overtime ended tied at 23.

The result marked the fifth time in 2012 that an Irish home game was decided by a TD or less. Here are more Notre Dame football notes:

- Notre Dame's 14-point, fourth-quarter comeback against Pitt marks its best at Notre Dame Stadium since 1999, when the Irish overcame a 14-point deficit against USC.
- Notre Dame is 5–0 this year in games decided by seven points or less. The school record is six games decided by seven or less (1939).
- Notre Dame ran off 104 total plays (87 in regulation), tying an all-time Irish single-game record. The Irish ran 53 pass plays, only the second time this season Notre Dame has thrown more times than it has run in a single game (the other against Purdue). In the fourth period and the three overtimes, Notre Dame ran 43 plays for 223 yards.

The Notre Dame sideline goes wild after Everett Golson scores from the 1-yard line in the third overtime to win the game.

- Notre Dame's 34 first downs were two short of the Irish single-game record.

Pittsburgh was the first time that we did not play with the same kind of physical and mental toughness that we had exhibited all year. Some early missed tackles. I remember the Pittsburgh team being able to run the football on us. We just didn't look like the same team. Offensively, we drove the ball down there. We were ineffective in the red zone and we kept them in the game.

The one thing that will be the mark of this 2012 team is they kept fighting. Regardless of the circumstances, they found themselves down late, kept fighting, kept playing. And we made that point to them at halftime. You're going to have to keep playing. It's four quarters, and don't look up, because if you look up, it's going to be too late.

They kept their heads down. They kept fighting. When it looked bleakest, they kept playing and found a way in overtime, three overtimes, to win a great ballgame.

—*Brian Kelly*

- The Irish defense in the fourth period and three overtimes allowed only 21 net yards on 23 plays. Pittsburgh's total offense in the three overtimes amounted to eight net yards.
- Pittsburgh's 308 net yards were 124 below the Panthers season average. Pitt entered the game converting 46 percent of its third downs but managed to convert only one time on 14 attempts against the Irish.
- Notre Dame has committed 11 turnovers this year combined over nine games—with 10 of the 11 occurring at Notre Dame Stadium.
- Notre Dame's win over Pittsburgh marked the first time in history the Irish have won a multiple-overtime game.
- Notre Dame is currently averaging 200.3 rushing yards and 204.1 passing yards per game. The only other seasons the Irish have been above the 200-yard mark in both categories were 1977 and 1970.
- Everett Golson now has run for 219 net rushing yards in 2012—while accounting for 230 net yards in the last five games combined.
- Golson had his hand on the football on 22 of Notre Dame's 25 plays against Pittsburgh in the fourth period. That included 17 pass attempts and five rushing attempts (one of those a two-point conversion run).
- If the Irish prevail at Boston College and move to 10–0, here are the previous seasons in which the Irish have started 10–0: 1924, 1930, 1949, 1973, 1988, 1989, and 1993.

We said early, we're good enough to beat anybody, and we're good enough to lose to anyone. And we're proving it on a weekly basis. We said that until January. We talked about how there are 12 winnable games on our schedule, but there are 12 losable games on our schedule.

So you've got Pittsburgh and you think you're riding high, and next thing you know, you're down 20–6 and you've already taken out your starter at quarterback, and now you're going to take out your backup.

Through all this is all the other things coach [Kelly] has been working on for three years—the mentality of handling adversity, playing through it, and playing together. Next-man-in mentality. Believing in kids. It doesn't matter who is out there; we're going to find a way to play and win games.

Like I said at one point in the fourth quarter, make sure they know we're going to win this game. We didn't think we had a better win than Norman. But when we go in this locker room, we're going to feel better, and sure enough, we did.

We didn't play as well, but it was still a win. To come back from 20–6 with your season on the line and do everything you can at times to lose a football game and still persevere and win. It says a lot about the character and togetherness of our team.

—*Chuck Martin*

Among those watching from the sideline today were former Irish standouts Chris Stewart and Ian Williams (he plays for the San Francisco 49ers).

Sunday, November 4

NBC's sixth Irish telecast of the season, featuring No. 3 Notre Dame's triple-overtime victory over Pittsburgh, earned a 4.3 overnight. That rating marked NBC's best Notre Dame metered market delivery this season, besting the 4.0 for Michigan, which aired in prime time. It was the best Notre Dame overnight on NBC since September 11, 2010, against

Michigan (4.5) and was also the highest for a game not vs. USC or Michigan in six-plus years, since September 9, 2006 (vs. Penn State, 4.8).

The NCAA's toughest schedule numbers this week list Notre Dame 23rd—with Irish opponents playing at a .577 rate (52–38) against FBS opposition. By comparison, Oregon ranks 25th, Kansas State 29th, and Alabama 33rd.

Late Saturday night, the Atlantic Coast Conference announced that ABC Sports would televise the Notre Dame–Boston College game next week from Boston. Irish fans had been frustrated that this was the one game of the year that went down to the wire in terms of announcement of the kickoff time—but Notre Dame's unbeaten status carried the game into a prime-time slot.

Tuesday, November 7

Here are the latest Heisman Trophy updates:

- The ESPN.com Heisman Watch has Notre Dame's Manti Te'o fourth (with 30 points), with its list of 15 experts featuring him behind Kansas State's Collin Klein (72 points), Oregon's Kenjon Barner (55), and Alabama's AJ McCarron (31).
- SI.com's Heisman Watch rates Te'o fourth behind Klein, McCarron, and Barner—though in actual voting of nine *Sports Illustrated* staffers, he's tied for second with Barner behind Klein.
- The CBSSports.com Heisman Watch lists Klein, Barner, McCarron, and Ohio State's Braxton Miller (in that order)—with Te'o and Texas A&M's Johnny Manziel in the others-to-watch category.

While Brian Kelly noted today that this may be new territory for the current Irish football team, a high BCS ranking late in the year is not foreign to Kelly. Just three years ago in 2009, his Cincinnati team finished 12–0 in the regular season and was ranked third in the final BCS poll, fourth in the USA Today/ESPN and Harris polls, and second in the computer rankings.

How about Notre Dame's margin of victory in 2012? It's an average of 28 points per game in four contests away from South Bend, compared to a 4.6 average (23 combined points) in five games at Notre Dame Stadium.

Todd McShay of ESPN.com recently rated the 10 most valuable players in college football, based on answering the question, "What would this team be like without this individual player?" McShay rated Kansas State's Collin Klein first and Ohio State's Braxton Miller second, with Notre Dame's Manti Te'o third. Here is what he wrote about Te'o: "Te'o was already a really good player coming into this season, but he has taken his game to the next level. He is quicker, after trimming down a bit this off-season, and he's diagnosing plays much faster. As a result, he's getting to plays earlier than he has in years past, and it's made a significant difference. Notre Dame has a lot of talent around him in that defensive front seven, but make no mistake: Te'o is the guy. He's the one who steps up and makes big plays when they need to be made, and he's played his best games in the team's biggest games. He's not just stuffing the run and making plays in the ground game—he's also become a major factor in the passing game. He has $1^{1}/_{2}$ sacks, 4 pass breakups, 4 QB hurries and 5 INTs this season. Based purely on talent, Te'o is one of the elite players in college football, and he'll go down as one of the best players to ever wear the Fighting Irish uniform. He is the emotional leader on a team that is 9–0 with the chance to go undefeated and play for a national championship. That's not a bad combination."

Mike Golic Jr. and Manti Te'o today were named to the Capital One Academic All–District V team. Both Golic and Te'o advance to the Capital One Academic All-America national ballot where first- and second-team honorees will be decided later this month. Golic graduated from the College of Arts and Letters in four years in May 2012 with a degree in film, television, and theatre and earned a cumulative GPA of 3.429. Te'o owns a 3.324 GPA as a design major in the College of Arts and Letters and will graduate this December after three and a half years.

In the latest *Sports Illustrated* issue, there's a two-page photo of Everett Golson in midair reaching the football over the goal line on the two-point conversion against Pittsburgh.

Saturday, November 10

While the Irish focus needed to be squarely on Boston College, the Notre Dame support staff hadn't missed the fact that Texas A&M had grabbed a 20–0 lead over top-rated Alabama just as the Irish team buses were headed to the game. And the usual pregame press box banter became muted, as virtually everyone became glued to the finish of the Tide-A&M matchup on CBS. In fact, once the Irish had beaten Boston College 21–6, there were just as many questions about Irish reaction to the Alabama loss as any other subject. Kelly and the Irish players interviewed in the stadium concourse all were queried about whether they had heard about the Tide defeat before the kickoff of the Notre Dame game.

While some of the buzz in Boston surrounded top-rated Alabama's first loss earlier in the evening to Texas A&M, fourth-ranked Notre Dame went about keeping its own title hopes alive in workmanlike fashion with the victory over old rival Boston College.

The win moved the Irish to 10–0 for their best start to a season since 1993—with Notre Dame left with Kansas State and Oregon as the only unbeaten bowl-eligible teams in the country.

Notre Dame won it in front of a prime-time audience on ABC and a sold-out Alumni Stadium crowd (44,500 fans) in the same manner it won games all year long—with a defense that kept the Eagles out of the end zone and a balanced offense that prevented Boston College from pulling off an upset in Kelly's return to his hometown area.

Irish quarterback Everett Golson enjoyed an efficient evening in completing 16 of his 24 throws for an even 200 yards. He threw for two touchdowns and ran for another on his way to 39 rushing yards.

Theo Riddick contributed 104 ground yards and four receptions for 56 yards, and Tyler Eifert paced the Irish receiving corps with six grabs for 67 yards. The Irish maintained control of this one by converting 11 of 14 third downs, including 10 straight to start the game.

Notre Dame set the tone on its very first possession of the game, using a 13-play march to go 95 yards for a 7–0 lead almost exactly halfway through the first quarter.

Riddick had 25 ground yards on that opening march to go with a 23-yard reception on a third-and-seven opportunity. Golson completed balls for 15 yards to Eifert and 14 to TJ Jones before running two yards for the TD.

Boston College came right back with a 69-yard drive of its own, finishing with a 36-yard Nate Freese field goal on the first play of the second quarter.

After a Notre Dame lost fumble, the Irish began again at their own 13 and this time traveled 87 yards in 16 plays over 8:30—with Golson finding backup tight end Troy Niklas for the seven-yard scoring play and a 14–3 Irish advantage. Golson completed five passes on that possession and Tommy Rees a sixth, as Notre Dame's score came with less than a minute remaining in the opening half.

The Irish took control by driving 65 yards in nine plays to start the third period. Golson did most of the damage himself, completing five more throws to four different receivers—including 18 yards into the end zone to a wide-open John Goodman for a 21–3 lead.

Boston College traveled to the Irish 39 before missing on a fourth-down throw. The following Eagles possession ended in a 45-yard Freese field goal just more than a minute into the final period, accounting for the final 21–6 score.

The final three Eagles attempts in the last period ended in a Kapron Lewis-Moore sack, a Manti Te'o interception (his sixth, for a Notre Dame record for linebackers), and a Prince Shembo fumble recovery.

Boston College quarterback Chase Rettig connected on 27 of his 43 throws for 247 yards, but the Irish held yet another opponent without a TD. The Eagles found themselves limited to 53 net rushing yards.

Notre Dame cornerback Bennett Jackson had eight tackles and safety Zeke Motta seven. Shembo contributed three sacks.

We thought Boston College was a trap game. We talked about it that way. Hey, this is the trap game. You're going on the road, Boston College. Here's a team that is 2–7, and you're going to make their season.

I thought we did a really good job, our players, of understanding what a trap game meant. We're going to have to play really good football. We didn't play outside ourselves. We didn't play too high; we didn't play too low. BC did what they needed to do. They took time off the clock and tried to control the ball, but it was very clean on our part. I don't think there was any time where we felt there was a panic or we didn't have the game in control. It was very professional. I use that word because of the way we went about it and did our business against BC.

—*Brian Kelly*

Boston College played pretty well against us. But we handled our business. Everett plays well again. He goes start to finish. Sometimes that part makes no sense—how well the kid performed on the road. It should be just the other way around. You go into a hostile environment, and I'll never forget it. I have no reason, and we talked about it a lot.

Efficient, blue-collar game at Boston College. Coach [Kelly] knows the history. Wouldn't be the first time they've ruined a great season at Notre Dame, if they want it more than we do. We physically handled our business. You could see we were getting better. We played the style we wanted to play to win games. We never got ahead of ourselves and said, now we can play fancy. Win the game in the trenches. Don't give up big plays. Our defensive front dominated the game like they always did.

—Chuck Martin

Sunday, November 11

Here are a few notes to know about Notre Dame linebacker Manti Te'o:

- Te'o has recorded six interceptions this year and is tied for second in the FBS in total interceptions.
- Te'o has set a Notre Dame record for most interceptions in a season by a linebacker.
- Only one FBS linebacker in the last 11 seasons has recorded more interceptions than the six tallied by Te'o (Tony Taylor, Georgia, seven in 2006).
- Te'o has started 46 career games at Notre Dame, including 45 consecutive contests. That is the longest streak of any linebacker in the nation and fourth-longest of any defensive player in the country.
- Only one player has recorded more takeaways this season than Te'o, who has generated eight turnovers (six interceptions and two fumble recoveries).

- Te'o has played a role in 10 of the 20 turnovers forced by Notre Dame's defense (six interceptions, two fumble recoveries and two hurried passes on plays directly resulting in interceptions).
- Te'o leads the Irish with 92 tackles and is on pace to become only the second Notre Dame player to ever record at least 100 tackles in three seasons (Bob Crable, 1979–1981).

Here are a few notes to know about Notre Dame football so far in 2012:

- The Irish are 10–0 for the eighth time in school history. Of the seven previous teams to open 10–0, five captured national championships and two others finished No. 2 in the nation.
- In the nine games played in November under coach Brian Kelly, Notre Dame is 8–1. In the nine November games prior to Kelly's arrival, the Irish were 1–8.
- Notre Dame has the No. 1 scoring defense in the nation, allowing 11.1 points per game. In the last 11 years, only seven FBS defenses have allowed fewer points per game than the Irish are currently allowing.
- Eight of the last 11 national champions ranked in the top eight nationally in scoring defense. Notre Dame is the only undefeated team ranked in the top 13 in scoring defense.
- Notre Dame opponents have started a drive at or inside their 40-yard line on 93 occasions this year. Only once has one of those possessions resulted in a touchdown (a three-play, 75-yard drive by Navy in the season opener).

Lastly, a few facts on notable Notre Dame football players:

- Quarterback Everett Golson is 8–0 as a starting quarterback and is tied with Terry Hanratty for the fourth-best start to a Notre Dame career. Only Kevin McDougal (9–0 in 1993), Frank Tripucka (9–0 in 1948), and Bob Williams (11–0 from 1949 to 1950) recorded more consecutive wins to start a career.
- Tight end Tyler Eifert needs five receptions to break Ken MacAfee's 35-year-old school record for most career receptions by a tight end. Eifert has 124 career catches for 1,625 yards.
- Left tackle Zack Martin has allowed one sack all year, and it came on the opening possession of the season. Martin leads the Irish with 123 knockdown blocks and grades out at a team-high 92 percent.
- Defensive end Stephon Tuitt has 11 sacks this year, which ranks him fourth nationally and second in Notre Dame history. Only Justin Tuck's 13^1/$_2$ sacks in 2003 are more than Tuitt's total this year. As a true sophomore, Tuitt leads the nation in sacks by an underclassman, and since 2005, only two underclassmen in the FBS averaged more sacks per game than Tuitt is currently averaging (Greg Middleton, Indiana, 2007, 1.23; George Selvie, USF, 2007, 1.12).

CBS drew an overnight rating of 6.6 for its coverage of Texas A&M's win over Alabama, the second highest-rated game on any network to date, behind CBS's coverage of Alabama-LSU (7.0). Notre Dame–Boston College drew a 3.8 overnight on ABC. Oregon-California was cable's top-rated cable college football game (2.4).

Monday, November 12

Notre Dame's Tyler Eifert today became one of eight semifinalists for the John Mackey Award that goes to the top tight end in the country. Finalists will be named next week.

Tuesday, November 13

The national colors will be presented prior to Saturday's Notre Dame–Wake Forest game by Nathan Hatch, president of Wake Forest University, and Reverend John I. Jenkins, C.S.C., president of Notre Dame, to celebrate the recently announced entry of Notre Dame into the Atlantic Coast Conference. Dr. Hatch, who served on Notre Dame's faculty for 30 years and was provost for the final nine, played a pivotal role in bringing the Irish into the ACC.

The 29 Notre Dame football senior players and their families will be introduced just prior to kickoff of the Notre Dame–Wake Forest game Saturday. That figures to be an emotional event for players and fans alike, given the Irish unbeaten status.

Our sales pitch is done on the field. When you get to Notre Dame, it speaks for itself. I spent four years there, and I just tell people my experience. They see the success that we've had on the football field. Combine that with the success we have in the classroom and the tradition and just the whole aura of the school. Walk through the locker room—movies are made about that locker room. Movies are made about that stadium. For me to run out of that tunnel for the first time, and then for me to run out of it for the last time—to be in a brighter spot than I was when I ran out of it the first time was definitely a big accomplishment not only for myself, but for the rest of the seniors and for our team.

—*Manti Te'o*

The Irish finished unbeaten at home in three straight football seasons in 1987 (5–0), 1988 (7–0), and 1989 (5–0). But since then Notre Dame's only home season without a loss came in 1998 (6–0). A win over Wake Forest Saturday would leave the Irish perfect at home in 2012 at 6–0.

Here are some of Brian Kelly's remarks to the media today:

- "A tangible goal for us this year was to protect our home field. If you want to take that next step in terms of success, you've got to win at home."
- On turnovers: "I don't believe it's an epidemic. I don't think it's a situation where we need to change anything. We just understand that turnovers in the game will affect our production."

Saturday, November 17

Linebacker Manti Te'o today was named one of four finalists for the 2012 Rotary Lombardi Award—not a bad way to start game day for the Notre Dame home finale. That came after Te'o was named on Thursday one of five finalists for the 2012 Bronko Nagurski Trophy, given to the best defensive player in college football by the Football Writers Association of America and the Charlotte Touchdown Club. But today was more about the final appearance in Notre Dame Stadium in 2012 for the Irish seniors.

Before the game started, third-rated Notre Dame celebrated its senior class, led by all-stars Manti Te'o and Tyler Eifert.

Once the contest began, the Irish worked their way to a surprisingly easy 38–0 victory over Wake Forest at Notre Dame Stadium, leaving Brian Kelly's still-unbeaten squad solidly in the national title conversation with only a finale at USC remaining for his team.

NBC televised the game, while 80,795 fans viewed in person.

The win enabled Notre Dame to finish unbeaten at home (6–0) for the first time since 1998 and reach the 11–0 mark for the first time since 1989. The Irish roared out of the gate and left only the final score in debate by halftime.

Kelly's team scored three touchdowns in the first 11 and a half minutes and led 31–0 at halftime.

Cierre Wood ran for 150 yards, including a 68-yard scoring dash less than two minutes into the contest.

Everett Golson threw a season-high three TD passes, two yards to Eifert in the first period, 50 yards to John Goodman later in the opening quarter, then 34 yards to TJ Jones midway through the second period. He threw for 346 yards overall (completing 20 of 30 throws), with 14 of his 17 tosses in the opening half producing first downs.

Notre Dame posted 430 total yards in the first half alone, including 317 passing yards by Golson (he was 17-of-25 in the first two periods).

Tyler Eifert hauls in a two-yard TD pass from Everett Golson in the first quarter of Notre Dame's 38-0 win over Wake Forest.

After two overtime wins at home and three other Notre Dame Stadium victories that came by a grand total of 13 points, this marked the most routine Irish outing since their 40-point win over Navy on opening day in Dublin.

Notre Dame amassed a season-high 584 total yards and held Wake Forest to 209. Eifert (85 receiving yards) and Jones (97) both caught six passes in the game. Eifert pushed his career receiving total to 130 to set the all-time Irish mark for tight ends.

Kelly brought his starting defensive unit off the field to a standing ovation with 13 minutes left in the contest and the issue long since decided. That came after an amazing first half in which the Irish had one three-and-out sequence but otherwise posted TD drives of 91, 52, 78, and 75 yards to go with a 51-yard excursion that ended in a field goal and another 70-yard possessions that ended when Golson threw an interception in the end zone.

It's an incredible group of young men to work with. Every single day, every play, every player, every day, everything they do is graded and inspected and feedback is given back to the players. It's so drilled down that we really don't sit back and relish in a team's success or a specific unit's success. It's just not that time frame.

—*Bob Diaco*

The Irish barely needed two minutes to get on the board—with Golson throwing 24 yards to Riddick, then Wood going 68 yards for a 7–0 lead. Carlo Calabrese forced a fumble that Zeke Motta recovered on the Demon Deacons' third play from scrimmage at the Notre Dame 48. That came after a 13-yard completion to leading rusher Josh Harris who was hurt on the play and did not return. Eight plays later, including a 20-yard Wood rush, Golson found Eifert in the end zone from the 2.

After a Wake Forest punt, Golson hit Riddick for 12 yards, Jones for 11, and then on first-and-10 located Goodman for 50 yards and a 21–0 lead with 4:28 remaining in the opening period.

After two more Demon Deacons punts, Golson fired 22 yards to Riddick, Wood ran for 16, then Golson connected with Jones for 34 yards to make it 28–0 at 6:17 of the second quarter.

After two more Wake Forest punts, Notre Dame took over with 2:47 left in the half and drove to the Demon Deacons 8, where Kyle Brindza knocked through a 25-yard field goal.

Notre Dame's 31–0 halftime margin featured a 430–113 edge in total offense, with the visitors limited to 15 net rushing yards in the opening two quarters.

The Irish missed a field goal on their opening possession in the third period, then closed the scoring on their next attempt. Wood's 43-yard rush marked the big play of the drive, and George Atkinson III went the last nine yards for the final 38–0 score.

Wake Forest finished with only nine first downs and 55 net rushing yards. The Irish forced 10 punts by the Demon Deacons. Notre Dame had not shut out a major-conference opponent in 10 years (since 42–0 over Rutgers in 2002). Calabrese and Louis Nix III both made seven tackles for Notre Dame, Te'o added six.

Wake Forest was going to be either a disaster emotionally, with everybody playing in their last game or it was going to be what it ended up being, and that was an enthusiastic capping of a great 2012 campaign for our seniors. Just the way the game unfolded offensively, we were able to hit big plays and get points on the board. What I remember most was being able to take a timeout, pull some of our key defensive players, and let that kind of be the memory. Taking our defensive players off the field at Notre Dame Stadium, where they had to make big, big plays the entire year, that's very unusual. I've only been able to do it one other time as the head coach…to take a timeout and let them really enjoy it. So that was a special moment.

—*Brian Kelly*

After more than its share of spine-tingling finishes, Irish players and coaches headed home Saturday evening after finishing off a perfect home season at Notre Dame Stadium with an emphatic 38–0 victory over Wake Forest. Little did they know what an evening it would turn out to be. As the clock ticked toward midnight, within a few minutes of each other, Kansas State and Oregon both went down to defeat, and it became apparent Notre Dame would rise to No. 1 in the polls. By the next morning, media questions all revolved around exactly where Brian Kelly and his players were, what they were doing, and what their reactions were as the top two teams in the polls both lost.

The next morning I have to be very careful, because we couldn't go into the game and let the BCS overshadow the opponent, USC. And I remember saying the three most important letters are not BCS here, but USC. Because if you think about BCS, USC will beat you.

—*Brian Kelly*

Tuesday, November 20

The Nassau County Sports Commission today named tight end Tyler Eifert a finalist for the John Mackey Award. It is the second consecutive season in which Eifert was named a finalist for the award presented to the nation's top tight end.

Here are a few notes to know about Notre Dame football:

- Notre Dame's defense is only allowing 10.1 points per game and is tied with Alabama for the best scoring defense in the nation. Over the last 10 years, only two FBS defenses have allowed fewer points per game than this year's Notre Dame defense.
- The Irish defense has allowed eight touchdowns all season, by far the fewest of any FBS team. The next closest is Alabama at 14 touchdowns allowed.
- Notre Dame leads the nation in fewest yards per pass completion.
- Notre Dame is 19–3 in its last 22 games. Only Oregon, Alabama, Northern Illinois, and Georgia have a better winning percentage since September 17, 2011.
- The Irish are one of three teams to average more than 200 rushing yards per game on offense *and* allow less than 100 rushing yards per game on defense. The other two are Alabama and Florida State.
- Notre Dame is the first school in the BCS era to be ranked No. 1 in both the current BCS standings and the current NCAA Graduation Success Rate rankings.

Here are a few notes to know about Notre Dame football players:

- Linebacker Manti Te'o is the only defensive player to be a finalist for the Maxwell Award. Te'o is also a finalist for the Bednarik, Nagurski, and Lombardi Awards. Previously named a National Scholar-Athlete because of his success in the classroom and commitment to the community, Te'o is also a finalist for the Campbell Trophy.
- Te'o needs two tackles to become the second Notre Dame player to record three consecutive seasons of at least 100 tackles.
- Te'o is on pace to lead the Irish in tackles for the third straight year. He would become the third Notre Dame player to accomplish that feat since 1956 (Bob Olson, 1967–1969; Bob Crable, 1979–1981).

- Only one FBS linebacker in the last 10 years has recorded more interceptions in a season than the six Te'o has totaled this year.
- DE Stephon Tuitt is tied for fourth in the nation with 12 sacks and trails Justin Tuck's school record of 13$\frac{1}{2}$ sacks with two games remaining.
- Nose guard Louis Nix III has played a vital role in helping the Irish rush defense this year. Notre Dame has the No. 5 rush defense in the nation at 92.2 yards per game and has permitted only two rushing touchdowns all season. Nix takes on multiple offensive linemen on almost every play, allowing Manti Te'o to run free and lead the team with 98 tackles. Despite facing constant double teams, Nix has totaled 42 tackles, 4$\frac{1}{2}$ tackles for loss, two sacks, four pass breakups, three QB hurries, and forced one fumble.
- Quarterback Everett Golson is 9–0 as a starter and is tied for the second best start to a Notre Dame career with Kevin McDougal (1993) and Frank Tripucka (1948). Golson trails only Bob Williams for most consecutive wins to start a career (11 from 1949 to 1950).
- Only six quarterbacks in Notre Dame history have ever thrown for more yards in a game than Golson, who passed for 346 yards vs. Wake Forest despite being pulled midway through the third quarter with a 38–0 lead. Only one first-year player at Notre Dame has ever passed for more yards in a game (Brady Quinn, 350 vs. Boston College in 2003, as a true freshman).
- The 317 passing yards in the first half by Golson is the most in a half since Jimmy Clausen set the school record with 340 passing yards in the second half vs. Navy in 2009. Golson is believed to set the school record for most passing yards in a first half.
- Notre Dame and USC have played football seven times in series history when the Irish were ranked No. 1. Notre Dame is 5–2 in those match-ups. The Irish last played the Trojans as the nation's top-ranked team

on November 26, 1988, when Notre Dame bested No. 2 USC 27–10, en route to a perfect regular season and eventual national championship.

- Notre Dame has entered its football season finale with USC undefeated and No. 1 in the nation with a national championship on the line on five previous occasions in school history (1938, 1947, 1964, 1966, and 1988). The Irish are 3–2 in those meetings. The defeats in '38 and '64 were the only setbacks for Notre Dame in those campaigns and cost the Irish national titles.

Thursday, November 22

The Irish practice early, enjoy Thanksgiving dinner together, then take the afternoon and evening off. It's very quiet on campus, with the vast majority of students home for the holiday break.

Friday, November 23

The Notre Dame traveling party takes its Delta charter into LAX, then heads to the Los Angeles Coliseum. With paint drying on the field, the Irish don't go through a full-scale workout, but they at least get a feel for the scene at one of college football's all-time great venues. Then it's off to their Marina del Rey hotel.

Saturday, November 24

There was no way to miss the significance—defeat USC and you are the only unbeaten team in the country and are destined to play for the BCS title. Lose to the Trojans, and your fate is unknown as part of a laundry list of one-loss teams. Here's how it went:

Top-ranked Notre Dame made use of a great, late goal-line stand to hold off a USC team led by first-time starting quarterback Max Wittek for a 22–13 Irish win at the Los Angeles Coliseum.

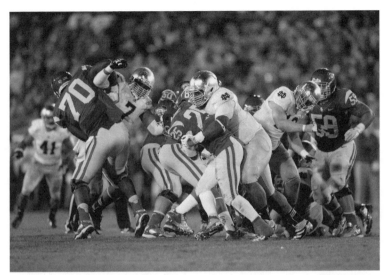

The Irish defense stifled USC's offense, shown here stopping Trojans running back Silas Redd (25).

ABC showed the game in prime time, while 93,607 fans came to USC's home facility

The victory ensured that the Irish—now at 12–0—would finish as the only unbeaten bowl-eligible team in the country, with Notre Dame destined to end up No. 1 in the final Bowl Championship Series standings and play for the national championship.

Brian Kelly's team never trailed, but late in the game USC appeared set to cut into the nine-point Irish lead, following a 43-yard kickoff return by Marqise Lee and a 53-yard completion to Lee from Wittek.

Consecutive interference penalties against Notre Dame set the Trojans up with a first down on the Notre Dame 1-yard line. Three runs produced nothing, and Wittek's fourth-down throw to fullback Soma

Vainuku came up short—and that set off the Irish celebration with 2:33 left in the game and the issue all but decided.

The goal-line stands are a function of players clearly knowing exactly what to do. It's players playing with whole heart, whole body, whole mind, being physically talented enough to get their job done and win their individual match-up at that particular moment.

They're cultural with our defense, the identity, the personnel, the vision, the family. Coach Kelly is about next man in—nothing will ever derail the energy, the program. It permeates through the defense, and we continue that same identity on the defense, in that no situation will be too much for us to take on, and no place on

Irish running back Theo Riddick breaks the plane of the Trojans' end zone, scoring Notre Dame's only touchdown in its 22–13 victory over USC.

the field will we get discouraged, no matter where the ball is placed. So you have that kind of energy, and then you say, hey, this is a great challenge. You have an opportunity to do something really special here, and your game rises.

—*Bob Diaco*

Theo Riddick made certain the Irish held their own offensively, gaining plenty of hard-earned real estate on his way to 20 carries for 146 yards and catching three balls for 33 yards. Kyle Brindza tied a Notre Dame record with five field goals, including a 52-yarder as time ran out at halftime for a 16–10 Irish lead.

Notre Dame played turnover-free football for the fourth time in 12 games, accounted for 222 rushing yards, and held the ball for more than nine minutes more than USC.

The Irish showed they meant business on their opening drive, advancing from their own 35 to the Trojans 9. Along the way Notre Dame utilized a 12-yard run by Riddick, a 22-yard Everett Golson throw to Robby Toma, a 12-yard Golson run, and a 13-yard Golson toss to TJ Jones. Brindza finished off the possession with a 27-yard field goal.

Notre Dame's lone touchdown of the evening came on its very next possession. Beginning at their own 13, the Irish watched as Golson completed three straight passes—11 yards to Riddick, 20 to Jones, and 15 to all-star tight end Tyler Eifert. That moved Kelly's squad from its own 30 to the USC 24. Golson again found Eifert for a dozen yards on third-and-nine, then Riddick ran nine yards for the score to make it 10–0 with 1:48 left in the first period.

Notre Dame notched 153 yards and 10 first downs in the first period and controlled the ball for 10:32.

USC's lone TD came on the next possession. Wittek hit Robert Woods for 18 yards and benefitted from two major penalties against the

Irish, with Wittek and Woods again hooking up from 11 yards out to make it 10–7 for the Irish five seconds into the second period.

The two teams traded field goals on subsequent possessions—Notre Dame going 67 yards (thanks to a 15-yard run by Riddick and a 15-yard Riddick reception) to set up a Brindza 29-yarder, and then USC traveling 54 yards for an Andre Heidari boot from 39.

After KeiVarae Russell intercepted a Wittek pass at his own 17 with 1:25 remaining in the opening half, Golson quickly threw to Wood for nine yards, John Goodman for 23, and Toma for a dozen. From the USC 35, Brindza closed the half with his 52-yard field goal that made it 16–10 Irish.

Manti Te'o got the Irish off to a strong second-half start by picking off Wittek on the second play from scrimmage. But Brindza misfired from 34 yards on a field-goal try. Neither team managed a first down until the Irish drove 70 yards late in the third period. Eifert hauled in a 36-yard reception to the USC 24, and Brindza pushed the margin to 19–10 with a 33-yarder at the 0:31 mark.

In the third period, Notre Dame limited USC to no first downs and 24 net yards.

The Trojans opened the final period with an 80-yard drive (Woods had grabs for 17 and 18 yards). The Irish defense stiffened after USC had a first down at the 4, and Heidari's field goal cut the lead to 19–13.

Notre Dame rebounded with a 39-yard George Atkinson III kickoff return to the Irish 44. Riddick ran 20 yards on first down, then had another rush for 15. Brindza's fifth three-pointer at 5:58 ended the scoring with the Irish on top 22–13.

That set the stage for the goal-line stand and sent the Irish home with their first perfect regular season in 24 years.

Notre Dame head football coach Brian Kelly celebrates with players in the locker room after their victory over USC completed a perfect 12–0 regular season, solidifying their No. 1 ranking and guaranteeing them a spot in the BCS title game in January.

The postgame scene was intense in a visiting locker room that was packed so tightly it was almost impossible to communicate. Brian Kelly's most noteworthy pronouncement? "We're going to South Beach." Kelly and Manti Te'o headed back to the field for interviews on the ESPN set that was on the edge of the field on the Notre Dame sideline. Many Irish fans stuck around to watch and celebrate. Then Kelly headed to a mobbed interview tent just outside the locker room. It was adequate, yet not really designed for an interview subject whose team just clinched a spot in the national championship game. A satisfied group of players headed up the Coliseum tunnel, grabbed burgers on the run from an In-N-Out truck, and then jumped on the buses.

Amongst all that noise, with us being ranked No. 1, I thought we did a great job all week in talking about USC, USC, USC. Our guys stayed focused on that. Our game plan really focused on what they had done all year and what they did against us last year that made it difficult for us. Having a new quarterback in there obviously gave our defense a lot of confidence that they could be aggressive.

There's a lot of pressure. You're going for an undefeated season. But our kids took the pressure, and I think they turned it into more than anything else a want and a desire to be undefeated more so than hoping to go undefeated. They wanted to go undefeated, and you could see that in their demeanor pregame.

There wasn't a lot of noise around here on campus that week because of the break and Thanksgiving. It allowed us to stay focused on having good practices, and I think it was probably aided by the break and not having a lot of people around.

—*Brian Kelly*

Sunday, November 25

It's a little eerie for the Irish players as they land at Michiana Regional Airport in the pre-dawn hours after flying all night from Los Angeles. The campus remains quiet as the players head home for some sleep. With no game next Saturday—and no known opponent in the BCS title game for another week—there are no Sunday meetings. Still, it's an ever-so-satisfying feeling to know the Irish are "in the clubhouse" in terms of the BCS title game.

We won the game in the trenches. Didn't give up plays. Our defensive front dominated the game like they always did. Our DBs did a great job like they did all year. Offensively, we stayed on the field and held them to nine possessions on offense. We felt like we were controlling the game the whole time. There was a brief moment where they got down to our 2, but our guys did a great job on the goal line. Every week it was taking advantage of what defenses were doing. We'd like to get to the point where we could do the dictating ourselves. We probably weren't at that stage in our offensive progression. Everett was growing up before our eyes and executed the game plan like a veteran.

—*Chuck Martin*

- With a 12–0 record, No. 1 Notre Dame (AP, *USA Today*) is one of only two FBS teams that finished the 2012 regular season undefeated. The other is 12–0 Ohio State (No. 4, AP), but the Buckeyes are not eligible for the *USA Today* poll.
- For only the second time in school history, Notre Dame has opened a season with 12 straight victories. The last time that happened was 1988, when the Irish won all 12 of their games en route to the national title.
- Among all-time Notre Dame head coaches, Lou Holtz and Brian Kelly are the only ever to post a 12–0 record.
- In 124 seasons of football beginning in 1887, Notre Dame has 13 unbeaten and untied seasons.
- Notre Dame has blanked nine of its 12 opponents in the first quarter this season. Miami, Oklahoma, and Pittsburgh are the only foes to score against the Irish in the opening 15 minutes (all field goals). The Irish have not surrendered a touchdown in the first quarter since November 26, 2011, against Stanford—a span that extends over 13 games.
- Notre Dame has outscored its opponents this season by an 85–9 margin in the first quarter.
- The nine points allowed in the first quarter are the lowest for Notre Dame in any quarter this season.
- That total marks the fewest points allowed in any quarter for Notre Dame since 1976 when the Irish allowed seven points in the opening quarter over the entire year.

- The 10 first-quarter points for Notre Dame were the most for the Irish at USC since November 26, 1988. The Irish raced out to a 14–0 lead after one quarter in that No. 1–vs.–No. 2 matchup.
- The Irish have been nearly as successful coming out of the halftime locker room. Notre Dame has outscored its opponents by a combined 67–17 in the third quarter. Pittsburgh scored 10 of those 17 points in the third quarter on November 3.
- Notre Dame has blanked 10 of its 12 opponents this season in the third quarter. In fact, the Irish have held 21 of their past 24 foes without an offensive score of any kind in the third quarter, dating back to the start of the 2011 season.
- Notre Dame limited USC to 24 total yards in the third quarter, including 10 on the ground and 14 through the air. Meanwhile, the Irish gained 102 total yards, including 66 on the ground and 36 through the air.
- The Irish now have won 15 consecutive games when rushing for at least 200 yards, with 222 tonight vs. USC. The Irish have not lost a game with more than 200 yards on the ground since November 3, 2007, against Navy.
- Notre Dame is 27–1 since the start of the 2002 season when it gains 200 or more yards rushing.
- Notre Dame has run for at least 200 yards seven times in 2012, including six of the past eight contests.
- The Irish have not posted more 200-yards-plus rushing games in a single season since 1996, when Notre Dame registered nine games with at least 200 yards rushing.
- Notre Dame has rushed for at least 200 yards 10 different times over the last two seasons—more than the previous five years combined (2006–2010).

- Over its past eight games, Notre Dame has combined to rush for 1,869 yards (340 attempts) for 5.5 yards per carry and 14 rushing TDs.
- Since the start of the 2005 season, Notre Dame has won 43 of its past 45 games when recording more rushing yards than its opponent (222–95 margin tonight vs. USC).
- Coach Brian Kelly has his own fairly remarkable run when his teams outrush their opponent. He now is 160–23–1 in his career and 22–2 at Notre Dame when winning the rushing battle.
- Te'o has seven interceptions this season, which leads the team, ranks second in the FBS, and leads all linebackers across the nation. He already owns the school record for interceptions by a linebacker in a single season.
- No FBS linebacker has recorded more interceptions in a single season over the past 13 years.
- No FBS linebacker has finished the year ranked higher in interceptions than sixth (Dan Dawson, Rice; 2000) over the past 13 years.
- Senior tight end Tyler Eifert hauled in a 36-yard pass from sophomore QB Everett Golson midway through the third quarter at USC to give him 1,779 yards receiving in his career. That moved him past Ken MacAfee (1,759) into first place on the all-time receiving yards list by an Irish tight end.
- 32 of Eifert's 44 catches this season have resulted in a touchdown or first down.
- Eifert leads the Irish with 12 receptions of at least 20 yards.
- Of his now 134 career catches, 29 have gone for at least 20 yards.
- Eifert ranks No. 1 in school history for career receptions (134) and career receiving yards (1,779) by a tight end.
- Sophomore quarterback Everett Golson has started 10 games in 2012 and led the Irish to victories in each contest. The 10 straight wins to

open his career as a starting quarterback is the second-most in school history. Bob Williams holds the school record as he guided Notre Dame to victories in his first 11 career starts.

Consecutive Wins to Open Career as Starting QB

1. Bob Williams (1949–1950) 11
2. *Everett Golson (2012) 10*
3. Kevin McDougal (1993) 9
   Frank Tripucka (1948) 9
5. Terry Hanratty (1966) 8
6. Matt LoVecchio (2000) 7
7. Rick Slager (1975) 6

- Golson came out of the locker room in the opening quarter at USC on fire. He completed seven of eight passes for 100 yards. His only incompletion was a throwaway on third down out of the end zone.
- After throwing for 317 yards in the first half last week against Wake Forest (most ever by a Notre Dame quarterback in the opening 30 minutes), Golson threw for another 181 yards in the opening half at USC. Golson now has thrown for 498 yards combined in the first half of Notre Dame's past two games (Wake Forest and USC).
- With the late goal-line stand at USC, the Notre Dame defense secured the ninth game this season in which it allowed one or fewer touchdowns by the opponent's offense (Purdue, BYU, and Pittsburgh each had two offensive TDs).
- Notre Dame's defense has allowed only two rushing touchdowns in 2012 (and the first did not come until the eighth game of the year against No. 8 Oklahoma on October 27). The Irish were the only team in the FBS that

did not allow a rushing touchdown over their first seven games of the 2012 season. Notre Dame still leads the FBS in fewest rushing touchdowns allowed.

- Notre Dame has given up exactly 11 rushing touchdowns over its past 30 games (dating back to the Tulsa game in 2010). Even more amazing, only four of those rushing touchdowns have come from an opposing running back, and two (Jonathan Lee's eight-yard TD run for Air Force with the Irish leading 59–27 with 33 seconds left in the fourth quarter on October 8, 2011, and D.J. Adams' two-yard touchdown on November 12, 2011, with the Irish leading Maryland 45–14 with 37 seconds left) came against the Irish reserves.
- Over the past 34 games, only five running backs have recorded a rushing touchdown against Notre Dame (Gee Gee Greene, Navy, 2010; Jon Lee, Air Force, 2011; Josh Harris, Wake Forest, 2011; D.J. Adams, Maryland, 2011; Ray Graham, Pittsburgh, 2012).
- The 11 rushing touchdowns allowed by Notre Dame over the past 30 games is tops in the FBS. Alabama is second with 12.
- Sophomore Kyle Brindza now is 23-for-31 on field goals for the season (and career). The 23 made field goals surpasses the single-season school record held by John Carney (21, 1986). Brindza is only the second place-kicker in school history to connect on at least 20 field goals in one season.
- Brindza's five field goals in a game is tied for the most in school history.
- Brindza belted a 52-yard field goal as time expired in the first half at USC to give Notre Dame a 16–10 lead.
- The 52-yard field goal is tied with David Ruffer (vs. Maryland, 2011) for the second-longest in school history. Dave Reeve (Pittsburgh, 1976) holds the school record with a 53-yard field goal.

- Brindza now owns the school record for field goal attempts in a single season with 31. He bested John Carney's previous mark of 28 from 1986.

We won 12 games because we could run the ball with the better teams on our schedule, and we could run the ball in the fourth quarter of games. We're going to have to win close games, and our schedule dictates there are always at least five or six really good teams that we're going to face. So how are we going to win when it counts? We were at our best in the fourth quarters of the games.

It's Coach Kelly's willingness to see how can we win here now. This is what we need to do, and it will always change. It's not major. It's a willingness to adapt and see. We knew what caused losing the first two years. We had turnovers. This year we were sixth in the country in turnovers. You don't have to look much further than that.

We were going to eradicate the turnovers from who we are and become a physical football team. We eradicated it for 365 days a year, just the emphasis on how to win games and not worry about looking fancy and flashy.

—*Chuck Martin*

Notre Dame's football team ranked No. 1 in the Associated Press poll for the second straight week today. It's the first time the Irish have ranked first in consecutive weeks since 1989, when the Irish started the campaign No. 1 and stayed there most of the regular season while winning their first 11 games that year.

Notre Dame today ranked 14th in the toughest schedule ratings released today by the NCAA (against FBS opponents only). The Irish opponents are 71–49 (.591). The top three teams on the list are Florida (.672), Missouri (.663), and California (.628). Second-rated Alabama is 29th (.558), and third-rated Georgia is 60th (.508).

Notre Dame finished its regular season ranked second in scoring defense (10.33, with Alabama first at 9.25); fifth in rushing defense

(92.42, behind Stanford, Alabama, BYU, and Florida State); and sixth in total defense (287.25, behind Alabama, Florida State, BYU, Michigan State, and Florida). Notre Dame has given up 10 touchdowns this season, best in the nation (Alabama is next with 14 allowed).

The Irish currently rank 27th nationally in rushing at 202.5 yards per game—the first time the Irish have been over the 200-yard mark since 2000 (213.5). With one game to go for Notre Dame, it's currently the first time since 1977 the Irish have averaged at least 200 yards both on the ground and through the air.

Notre Dame's Manti Te'o now has seven interceptions this year and is tied for second nationally in that category. The only player with more is Phillip Thomas of Fresno State with eight. The next linebacker on the list is Oregon's Kiko Alonso, tied for 30th with four.

Here's where current Irish players rank on NCAA career lists for active players:

- Manti Te'o: 2nd in total tackles (427); Ball State's Travis Freeman is 1st (455)
- Manti Te'o: 4th in assisted tackles (218)
- Manti Te'o: 6th in solo tackles (209)
- Manti Te'o: 9th in tackles per game (8.5)
- Manti Te'o: 9th in assisted tackles for loss (18)
- Kapron Lewis-Moore: 9th in assisted sacks (6)
- Theo Riddick: 8th in all-purpose yards per play (8.53)
- Stephon Tuitt: 10th in sacks per game (0.6)

Notre Dame finished 15th among FBS schools in attendance this year—with six sellouts giving the Irish an average of 80,795 at Notre Dame Stadium.

At this point we know we're playing for a national championship, even if we don't know who we play. We actually went out and did some recruiting, and then set our schedule. That was a memorable night when we were on the selection show. Notre Dame playing for a national championship is why we're all here.

—Brian Kelly

Chapter 8

Run-up to the BCS

Saturday, December 1

Manti Te'o was announced Thursday as winner of the 2012 Awards and Recognition Association Sportsmanship Award, given annually to one outstanding NCAA Division I collegiate football player who best personifies the spirit of sportsmanship.

Notre Dame assistant head coach/defensive coordinator/linebackers coach Bob Diaco has been named one of five finalists for the Broyles Award, announced recently by the Rotary Club of Little Rock. The Broyles Award honors the top assistant college football coach in America. In addition to Diaco, the finalists include: Georgia offensive coordinator Mike Bobo, Florida defensive coordinator Jeff Quinn, Texas A&M offensive coordinator Kliff Kingsbury, and Stanford defensive coordinator Derek Mason. The 2012 Broyles Award winner will be announced Tuesday in Little Rock, Arkansas.

Te'o has been named to the 2012 All-America first team by the American Football Coaches Association and was also selected among five finalists for the Walter Camp Football Foundation Player of the

Year Award. Te'o would be the first exclusively defensive player to win the Player of the Year Award since Hugh Green of Pittsburgh in 1980. Te'o becomes Notre Dame's 186th All-America first-team selection.

Sunday, December 2

It's official. Even though the Irish have known for a week they have earned their way into the title game, they now know that Alabama will be the opponent after the Tide's comeback win over Georgia Saturday in the Southeastern Conference Championship Game in Atlanta. With the history between Notre Dame and Alabama, there will be no shortage of storylines in the next five weeks.

The entire team and staff and their families gather in the Gug auditorium to watch the BCS selection show live—with Brian Kelly doing several live shots during the show. The players all wear shirts that say "Unfinished Business."

Kelly makes it clear that he challenged the players not to simply celebrate the accomplishments of their 12–0 regular season. "Are we going to stop here, or are we going to finish it off?" asked Kelly.

Monday, December 3

The Football Writers Association of America, in conjunction with the Fiesta Bowl, announced today that Notre Dame coach Brian Kelly is one of nine finalists for the 2012 Eddie Robinson Coach of the Year Award, whose winner will be revealed December 13.

Notre Dame linebacker Manti Te'o claimed the 2012 Bronko Nagurski Trophy tonight in Charlotte, North Carolina. The 6'2", 255-pound senior became the 20th winner of the trophy, which annually is awarded to the best defensive player in college football as voted upon by the FWAA. Te'o received the award at a banquet at the Westin Hotel, sponsored by the Charlotte Touchdown Club.

"It's definitely a great accomplishment for me." Te'o said after receiving the trophy. "I've ways wanted to be the best. For this to happen helps me to know I'm heading in the right direction. The formula is the same: hard work leads to success as long as I keep doing it."

Coincidentally, his head coach was the keynote speaker at the banquet. Te'o is the first Notre Dame player to win the Bronko Nagurski Trophy and only the second finalist from the school.

The Heisman Trust announced its three finalists for this year's Heisman Trophy race tonight on ESPN's 6:00 PM edition of *SportsCenter*. The gridiron stars in contention for the prestigious 78th Annual Heisman Memorial Trophy are Kansas State University quarterback Collin Klein, Texas A&M University quarterback Johnny Manziel, and University of Notre Dame middle linebacker Manti Te'o.

The three finalists will be invited to New York for the live Heisman Trophy announcement on Saturday. Each finalist would be accomplishing a notable first as the 2012 Heisman Trophy winner: first from Kansas State, first freshman, or first true defensive player to ever be named the year's outstanding college football player.

Klein would be the first Kansas State Wildcat to win the Heisman Trophy. Klein passed for 2,490 yards and 15 touchdowns and rushed for 890 yards and 22 touchdowns. The senior holds the Football Bowl Subdivision record of the most rushing touchdowns in two seasons, totaling 49 between 2011 and 2012. Klein ranks second in Kansas State history for scoring with 336 points and third in career yards with 7,028.

Manziel would be the first-ever freshman Heisman Trophy winner. Hailing from Texas A&M, the young quarterback passed for 3,419 yards and 24 touchdowns. He also rushed for 1,181 yards and 19 touchdowns. Manziel is the first quarterback in SEC history, and only the fifth player ever in the NCAA Football Bowl Subdivision, to have 3,000 passing yards and 1,000 rushing yards in the same season. Upon surpassing 4,600 yards, he set a new SEC record for total yards in a season. Manziel holds a Texas A&M record of logging eight straight games with 300 or more total yards.

Te'o would be the first true defensive player to ever win the award, joining seven previous Notre Dame players as a Heisman Trophy winner. This season, Te'o helped lead the Fighting Irish to an undefeated season with 101 tackles, of which 46 were solo tackles; he ranks third in Notre Dame history for career tackles at 427. Te'o amassed a school-record of seven interceptions in his third-straight 100-plus tackle season.

Te'o also was honored with the 28th annual collegiate Butkus Award today. The announcement came in a surprise telephone call from legendary linebacker and award namesake Dick Butkus and his son, Matt. Te'o was selected by a panel of 51 coaches, recruiters, scouts, and journalists coordinated by *Pro Football Weekly*. "Manti Te'o embodies the toughness, intensity, competitiveness, and on-field demeanor of a throwback performer like Dick Butkus himself," said Hub Arkush of *Pro Football Weekly*. "Te'o was the first-ever High School Butkus winner [2008], and he has lived up to all the expectations and positioned his team for a chance at the national championship. He has been an inspiration to his team and community and serves as a model citizen." Te'o finished with 83 points in the Butkus Award voting system. Finishing second was Jarvis Jones of Georgia (54 points), and third was C.J. Mosley of Alabama (21 points). Kevin Minter of LSU and Dion Jordan of Oregon were tied for fourth.

Meanwhile, Notre Dame athletics staffers were in New York, hosting a dinner at the Penn Club to honor Notre Dame's College Football Hall of Fame inductee, Dave Casper.

Tuesday, December 4

It's a big Irish night at the Waldorf-Astoria in New York, as Dave Casper officially enters the College Football Hall of Fame and Manti Te'o continues his hectic awards-circuit tour as he's honored as a National Football Foundation Scholar-Athlete.

Meanwhile, Notre Dame assistant head coach/defensive coordinator/linebackers coach Bob Diaco is in Little Rock, Arkansas, as he wins the Broyles Award as the nation's top assistant coach, announced tonight by the Rotary Club of Little Rock.

Here is a list of accomplishments from Diaco's defense in 2012:

- Notre Dame ranks first in the FBS in scoring defense—allowing just 10.3 points per game. The Irish are one of just three scoring defenses in the top 10 of the FBS to exclusive FBS competition. Notre Dame has allowed 10 touchdowns this season (only nine offensive touchdowns)—seven fewer than any other FBS school. Florida has surrendered 17. Notre Dame has allowed 28 total scores (10 TDs and 18 FGs), while Alabama has allowed 23 (18 and five).
- Notre Dame has allowed 124 combined points over its 12 games this season. The Irish have never surrendered fewer points over their first 12 games of a season in school history.
- The Irish have allowed six offensive touchdowns over their last 10 games.
- Notre Dame has held six opponents without an offensive touchdown and nine foes to one or fewer offensive touchdowns.

- Notre Dame has limited 10 opponents to 14 points or less. The Irish have not held more foes to 14 points or less in a single season since 1921.

Wednesday, December 5

Manti Te'o won the Rotary Lombardi Award in Houston tonight as college football's best lineman or linebacker. He is the second player in college football history to capture the Butkus, Nagurski, and Lombardi awards in the same season.

Thursday, December 6

The accolades continue to roll in for members of the top-ranked Notre Dame football team. Graduate student Mike Golic Jr. (West Hartford, Connecticut) and senior Manti Te'o (Laie, Hawaii) today were selected as first-team members to the Capital One Academic All-America Football Team which is selected annually by CoSIDA (College Sports Information Directors of America).

Notre Dame's Tyler Eifert won the John Mackey Award that goes to college football's best tight end. Coming into the season, Eifert was regarded as the best receiver for the Fighting Irish and drew extra attention from opposing defenses. Nonetheless, Eifert had 44 receptions for 624 yards and four touchdowns as the top-ranked Irish finished the season unbeaten.

The awards circuit moves to the Boardwalk at Disney World in Orlando, Florida, tonight as the Home Depot Coach of the Year Award is presented to Notre Dame's Brian Kelly as a part of the Home Depot College Football Awards on ESPN. Kelly also was named the recipient in 2009, coaching for Cincinnati, and is the first two-time winner of the award. In his third season at Notre Dame, he is the first Irish coach since ESPN analyst Lou Holtz's 1994–1996 seasons to register winning records over three straight seasons. Kelly's Irish have won at least eight games in each of his first three seasons on the Notre Dame sideline. That record surpasses the record of Lou Holtz, Ara Parseghian, Frank Leahy, and Knute Rockne, who combined to win 10 consensus national championships.

Parseghian is recognized during the show with the NCFAA Contribution to College Football Award. He is the subject of an emotional feature that highlights both his coaching achievements as well as his work to defeat the deadly Niemann-Pick Type C disease that afflicted three of his grandchildren. Parseghian is joined by his wife Katie, son Mike, and daughter-in-law Cindy (Cindy and Mike have headed the Ara Parseghian Medical Foundation) in the front row for the show. After the video feature, he joins ESPN's Tom Rinaldi on stage and delivers stirring remarks that earn him a standing ovation.

Another highlight comes earlier in the afternoon when Parseghian joins Kelly and Holtz in a taped interview from an outdoor balcony at the Boardwalk. With Rinaldi moderating, the trio discusses all things Notre Dame—and that becomes a half-hour feature on ESPN later in the month.

Eifert receives the Mackey Award as part of the red-carpet ceremonies, while Te'o wins the Walter Camp and Maxwell Player of the Year Awards and the Bednarik Award.

Friday, December 7

Here's where Manti Te'o has been this week—Charlotte Monday, New York Tuesday, Houston Wednesday, Orlando Thursday, New York again Friday. On this trip to New York, at least Te'o and his parents are in the same city two nights in a row, thanks to his invitation to the Heisman Trophy proceedings this weekend.

With Kansas State's Collin Klein in Baltimore to receive the Johnny Unitas Award, Te'o and Texas A&M's Johnny Manziel were the only two finalists in New York today. They left about 8:30 AM from Orlando, arriving on a flight that featured photos all around with a Heisman Trophy once they landed in New York. After a casual lunch at Tony DiNapoli's in Times Square, both candidates took part in a jam-packed media session at the Marriott Marquis. They took lots of photos with the trophy, individually and together. Then it was off to the ESPN bus to do more interviews. To start the evening, both players appeared at the Wendy's High School Heisman dinner—among those also attending was former Irish Heisman winner John Lattner. Then it was off to 30 Rock where Manti and his parents taped interviews for NBC's December 22 season review show. Then they all watched the Notre Dame football awards show via UND.com from a sixth-floor green room—and Manti did a live shot back to the show after winning the MVP award. Finally it was off to the Terrace Club for a reception with Heisman friends and sponsors. Among those in attendance was former Irish Heisman winner Tim Brown. Manti's father, Brian, met Brown, shook his hand, and promptly offered, "I'm never going to wash that hand again."

Meanwhile, with Te'o in New York, the rest of the Notre Dame football family headed to the DeBartolo Performing Arts Center on campus for the 92nd Notre Dame Football Awards Ceremony (Echoes). Te'o was selected the 2012 Notre Dame Monogram Club Most Valuable Player in a vote by members of the Notre Dame team and was one of 19 players honored at the show sponsored by the Notre Dame Club of St. Joseph Valley.

Senior tight end Tyler Eifert and senior safety Zeke Motta were named Notre Dame's offensive and defensive players of the year, respectively.

Senior wide receivers John Goodman and Robby Toma shared the Nick Pietrosante Award. The Pietrosante Award is given to the student-athlete(s) who best exemplified the courage, loyalty, teamwork, dedication, and pride of the late Irish All-America fullback. Pietrosante, Notre Dame's leading rusher in 1957 and 1958 (and later a No. 1 draft pick and two-time Pro Bowl selection with the Detroit Lions), died of cancer on February 6, 1988. The recipient is determined by a vote of the players, and past winners have included Robert Hughes, Mike Anello, Tom Zbikowski, John Carlson, Jeff Faine, Harrison Smith, Aaron Taylor, and Chris Zorich.

Senior offensive tackle Zack Martin won the Offensive Lineman of the Year. He is the first player in Notre Dame history to win the award three times.

Junior nose guard Louis Nix III and sophomore Stephon Tuitt shared the Lineman of the Year Award presented by the Moose Krause Chapter of the National Football Foundation and Hall of Fame.

Junior quarterback Tommy Rees captured the Next Man In Award. He has come off the bench for Notre Dame in seven separate games in 2012. Rees has completed 64.1 percent of his passes for 294 yards and one touchdown as a non-starter.

The Offensive Newcomer of the Year Award was presented to sophomore quarterback Everett Golson. He has started 10 games in 2012 and led the Irish to victories in each contest.

Freshman cornerback KeiVarae Russell was presented with the Defensive Newcomer of the Year Award. He was the first freshman ever at Notre Dame to start at cornerback in the opening game of a season (September 1 against Navy).

Sophomore Kyle Brindza earned the Special Teams Player of the Year Award. He is 23-for-31 on field goals this season (and career). The 23 made field goals not only leads the FBS but also surpasses the previous single-season school record held by John Carney (21, 1986).

Here are the final awards of the evening: Offensive Scout Team Player of the Year (Nick Fitzpatrick), Defensive Scout Team Player of the Year (Tyler Stockton), Irish Around the Bend Award (Mike Golic Jr.), A-Team Award (Kapron Lewis-Moore), Count on Me Award (Theo Riddick), Father Lange Iron Cross Award (Braxston Cave), and Rockne Student-Athlete Award (Danny Spond).

Saturday, December 8

Today the Heisman finalists headed back to the ESPN bus at 9:45 AM, then went to a walk-through at Best Buy Theatre for tonight's event. They taped interviews at CBS for halftime of the Army-Navy game today (with former Irish star Aaron Taylor of CBS) and then had a 5:45 PM press conference at the Marquis prior to the show at 8:00 PM.

After all the hoopla, Te'o finished second at the 2012 Heisman Trophy ceremony. He is the third solely defensive player to finish in the top two of the Heisman Trophy balloting and the first since Pittsburgh defensive end Hugh Green in 1980. Iowa defensive tackle Alex Karras was the runner-up in 1957.

Including Notre Dame's seven previous winners, Te'o is the 17th Irish player to finish in the top three (11th in the top two). It's the highest a Notre Dame player has finished since 1990 when flanker Raghib Ismail was runner-up to BYU quarterback Ty Detmer. Te'o was Notre Dame's first Heisman Trophy finalist since quarterback Brady Quinn in 2006. Quinn finished third in that year's balloting.

Texas A&M redshirt freshman quarterback Johnny Manziel edged out Te'o. Kansas State signal-caller Collin Klein finished a distant third. Te'o finished with 321 first-place votes and 1,706 points—the most ever by a defensive player in college football history. Te'o has captured the Nagurski Trophy, Butkus Award, Lombardi Award, Bednarik Award, Maxwell Award, and Walter Camp Player of the Year. He is the first player in college football history to sweep the aforementioned six awards. In fact, no other player in college football history has ever captured more than five major awards in one season.

Te'o was named on 84 percent of the ballots (Manziel on 92)—compared to 2011 when Robert Griffin II was named on 80 percent and Andrew Luck was named on 75 percent.

Te'o nearly became the third player to ever be named a first-team Academic All-American and win the Heisman in the same year—he would have joined Pete Dawkins (Army) in 1958 and Danny Wuerffel (Florida) in 1996.

At the presentation Saturday night, siting in the front row next to Te'o were four of Notre Dame's previous Heisman winners—Tim Brown, John Lattner, John Huarte, and Paul Hornung. Traveling into New York Saturday afternoon for the event were athletics director Jack Swarbrick, head coach Brian Kelly, and defensive coordinator Bob Diaco.

Te'o's parents, Brian and Ottilia, have been along every step of the way on the awards presentation circuit this week—beginning Monday in Charlotte (Manti won the Nagurski Award), Tuesday in New York (National Football Foundation National Scholar-Athlete), Wednesday in Houston (Lombardi Award), Thursday in Orlando (Walter Camp and Maxwell Player of the Year Awards, as well as Bednarik), then Friday and Saturday back in New York for the Heisman Trophy events. Sunday morning, Manti and his parents and coach Brian Kelly headed to Newport Beach, California, for that evening's presentation of the Lott IMPACT Award.

Manti's father, Brian, passed out lots of leis at the ceremonies Saturday and wore Kukui nuts around his own neck—also presenting garlands to Manziel's parents, Paul and Michelle. Manti also invited the Manziels to visit him and his family in Hawaii—and long after the announcement was over, Michelle in the Heisman hospitality suite said she had no plan to take off her lei and she had every intention of taking the Te'os up on their offer to visit Hawaii. Brian spent much of the week recording the events and presentations on his iPad.

Meanwhile, it will be a quiet week on the Irish athletics front with final exams beginning Monday and running through Friday.

Our preparation for the BCS game was good. The plus was we were No. 1 for 42 days. That helped us finish out a great recruiting class. Some of what we accomplished, you kind of have time to look up and appreciate it. You knew the daunting task that lay ahead—we watched the tape, and we knew it anyway. We knew certain things had to go our way that night. We were fully planning on, hey, whether we're the better team or not, we're going to find a way to do it.

—*Chuck Martin*

Friday, December 14

Manti Te'o became the 33rd unanimous All-American in Notre Dame history when he was selected to the 2012 Football Writers Association of America (FWAA) All-America Team today. He is the first Irish defensive player to earn such an honor since cornerback Shane Walton in 2002. Te'o was a first-team All-American on all five teams the NCAA recognizes to calculate unanimous All-America standing. He was previously selected to the All-America squads by the American Football Coaches Association, *Sporting News*, the Walter Camp Football Foundation, and the Associated Press. Te'o is Notre Dame's fourth-ever unanimous All-America linebacker and first since Michael Stonebreaker in 1990—also joining the likes of Jim Lynch (1966) and Bob Golic (1978).

Meanwhile, Notre Dame coach Brian Kelly, who has taken the Fighting Irish to their first unbeaten regular season since 1988, has been named the recipient of the 2012 FWAA/Eddie Robinson Coach of the Year Award, which is sponsored by the Fiesta Bowl. Kelly won the award over eight other coaching finalists after a vote of the 1,200-member Football Writers Association of America. He is the fourth Notre Dame coach to receive the award following Ara Parseghian (1964), Lou Holtz (1988), and Charlie Weis (2005). Kelly will be presented the Eddie Robinson Trophy during a reception at the Marriott Harbor Beach Hotel in Fort Lauderdale, Florida. Officials from Notre Dame, the Fiesta Bowl, the FWAA, and the namesake coach's son, Eddie Robinson Jr., will be in attendance.

Monday, December 17

Monday was a memorable day for 100 youths from the South Bend area as well as 100 football players from the University of Notre Dame. The Kelly Cares Foundation, the charity founded by Fighting Irish head football coach Brian Kelly and his wife, Paqui, donated $10,000 to create 100 gift cards worth $100 to Meijer.

The underprivileged kids from St. Joseph County ranged from fourth to eighth grade and were paired with members of Notre Dame's football team for the shopping spree. The children met the football players at the Guglielmino Athletics Complex on Notre Dame's campus before traveling with their player to Meijer on buses donated by Royal Excursion. The kids were allowed to purchase anything they wanted with the gift card.

"I frequently talk to our team about accountability, appreciation, and achievement," Brian Kelly said. "It's so critical—especially at this time of the year—to have appreciation for all you have. One way we try to build appreciation in our program is through our Irish Around the Bend initiative that gets our players in the local community. Today was one of the largest and most successful experiences our players have had to date."

Following the shopping spree, the kids and Notre Dame football team had dinner together at Papa Vino's, a local Italian restaurant, before returning to their respective homes. Papa Vino's donated the meals for the children.

Today also was media day for the BCS Championship Game—as Brian Kelly, his players, and assistants were available to the press corps. It was the best chance for national and Alabama media to come to South Bend to gain access to the Irish before the trek to South Beach. And the Gug auditorium was packed with cameras and people for the Kelly interview, before everyone moved to tables in the Loftus Center to meet with the players and assistants.

Lindy's has published a special edition on Notre Dame football titled *Waking Up the Echoes*, with Manti Te'o on the cover. *Sports Illustrated* has produced a special BCS preview issue, with Te'o on the cover of the Notre Dame–area edition.

Stewart Mandel of *Sports Illustrated* ranked his top 10 moments from college football in 2012 and rated the Irish season second: "Notre Dame's renaissance. The Fighting Irish were never 'irrelevant'; they just weren't very good for the past 18 seasons. In fact, I devoted untold column space over those years to the struggles and drama surrounding the Bob Davie, Tyrone Willingham, and Charlie Weis eras, respectively. It's much more fun, both for those of us who cover the sport and for longtime fans of college football, when Notre Dame is making news for winning football games. And it's even more interesting that this year, the Irish returned to national championship

contention not behind a 40-points-per-game offense like the ones
Brian Kelly employed at Cincinnati, but thanks to an old-school,
hard-nosed defense led by standout linebacker Manti Te'o. There were
times over the years when it seemed unlikely a midwestern private
school playing an independent schedule could ever again reach the
heights it so often enjoyed from the 1920s to '80s. But now that it's
happened—and now that the nation once again associates those gold
helmets with elite-level football—it feels only natural. It's as if the
Irish were here all along."

Sports Illustrated also rated its top 112 moments of the past year in
all sports and has the Irish 10th: "NOTRE DAME RETURNS TO GLORY—
Notre Dame's magical season started in Dublin, Ireland. It will end
in an even more unexpected location: South Florida for the BCS title
game. The Irish started the season unranked in the AP poll for the
seventh time in 11 seasons. But in Brian Kelly's third season in South
Bend, Notre Dame survived a difficult schedule (winning road games
at Michigan State, Oklahoma, and USC) and some close calls (beating
Stanford in overtime and outlasting Pittsburgh in three OTs) to climb
to No. 1 in the polls for the first time since 1993 and atop the BCS
standings for the first time. Now only SEC power Alabama stands
in the way of the Irish's 14th—and arguably most unlikely—national
championship."

Irish coach Brian Kelly met the media after today's Notre Dame
football practice at the Loftus Center and said today's and tomorrow's
workouts would be the most intense physical practices of Notre Dame's
preparation for the BCS Championship Game. Kelly termed today's
work the most contact the Irish have had since the finale against USC
more than a month ago. "We've kept timing and conditioning as the
focal points for the older guys, and a lot of the young guys got a lot

of good work in our earlier practices. Now it's all about Alabama. We did some 11-on-11 work today (for 10 minutes) with the ones against the ones, just to keep up the speed you need against a team like Alabama."

Kelly informed the media that receiver DaVaris Daniels returned at full speed today and said, "He'll play a role in the game."

Kelly praised the Tide, saying, "If you say you're just going to play the game between the tackles, you're in for a long day. You've got to use the field. We've got to get some chunk plays. We know that. They know that. Up front Alabama is athletic at 290 pounds. They are disciplined and well-coached. There's not one of their guys where you say, 'Let's go attack him.' They are just a good football team from one to 11 on offense and defense."

Kelly suggested he may flip some personnel on special teams, calling it a "one-shot-deal, all-hands-on-deck" situation.

Kelly also noted that maybe at past bowl games, he would give his players a 2:00 AM curfew the first few nights at the bowl site: "We'll have an 11:00 PM curfew. This is not a bowl game. This is for the national championship. We're there on a business trip, it's not to enjoy South Beach."

Kelly was asked if he could see this coming three years into his tenure at Notre Dame and replied, "I didn't think we couldn't [do it]. I didn't see any impediment. There wasn't anything here that said we couldn't do it."

Wednesday, December 19

Brian Kelly adds another national Coach of the Year honor to the list as the Associated Press announces that award. It's the first time an Irish football coach has won the AP award.

"When you're talking about the Coach of the Year, there's so many things that go into it," Kelly said. "I know it's an individual award and it goes to one guy, but the feeling I get from it is you're building the right staff, that you've got the right players, and to me that is a validation of the program. That you put together the right business plan."

Kelly received 25 votes from the AP college football poll panel. Penn State's Bill O'Brien was second with 14 votes. Stanford's David Shaw (four), Texas A&M's Kevin Sumlin (three), Kansas State's Bill Snyder (two), and Alabama's Nick Saban (one) also received votes.

The Irish practiced through December 21 on campus—then the players were excused as of 1:00 PM to head home. The Irish squad reconvened for a 3:00 PM team meeting on December 27—and followed that with a weightlifting session, meetings, and a walk-through.

Friday, December 28

The Irish had a noon special-teams meeting and walk-through followed by hour-long position meetings and then an hour-and-50-minute practice in Loftus Center. After dinner at a local restaurant, the Notre Dame team went bowling.

Saturday, December 29

The Irish had a 1:00 PM special-teams meeting and walk-through, followed by position meetings and another hour-and-50-minute workout in full pads. After practice Kelly and a handful of players met the media for the last time before the team heads to Florida.

Sunday, December 30

The Irish had another full-contact practice, following the same timing pattern as the previous two days.

Monday, December 31

After meetings, the Irish practiced for an hour and 20 minutes, followed by a 2:45 PM lunch. The entire team of players, coaches, and staff met at Legends, just south of Notre Dame Stadium, for a New Year's Eve party.

Tuesday, January 1

The Irish held a late-morning weightlifting session, meeting, and walk-through and were done for the day by 1:30 PM.

Chapter 9

South Bend to South Beach

Wednesday, January 2

The top-rated Irish are headed to South Florida today for next Monday's BCS Championship Game against second-ranked Alabama. Notre Dame's Delta charter will be more crowded than usual since the entire Irish football squad and traveling party will be traveling together from South Bend. Normally, based on an earlier game date, the players would head home for a Christmas break, then fly individually to the bowl site.

The Notre Dame football charter arrived right on time in South Florida (3:45 PM)—and the Irish were met with a water cannon welcome, lots of Orange Bowl reps in their bright blazers, and dozens more media and cameras.

The Irish are traveling this week in buses wrapped with photos of the Notre Dame players and coaches, and it didn't take long for coach Brian Kelly to get a sense of the interest in the BCS title game, as he stood beside one of the buses, surrounded by far more cameras than could record the proceedings. Irish receiver Robby Toma also spoke to the media—with a number of alumni from the local Notre Dame club also part of the receiving party.

Florida Sports played host to a two-hour welcome reception for the Irish staff and families at the Westin Diplomat—including remarks from Orange Bowl officials as well as Kelly and athletics director Jack Swarbrick. Meanwhile, the Irish players had a quick dinner at the hotel and a team meeting, then headed out to see the NBA's Miami Heat meet the Dallas Mavericks (the Heat won 119–109). Irish lineman Louis Nix took part in a special timeout event.

Meanwhile, Kelly today was named the Walter Camp 2012 Coach of the Year. The Walter Camp Coach of the Year is selected by the nation's 124 Football Bowl Subdivision head coaches and sports information directors. Kelly is the first Notre Dame coach to receive the award.

Thursday, January 3

At 8:30 this morning, a contingent of defensive coordinator Bob Diaco and players Manti Te'o, Kapron Lewis-Moore, Danny Spond, Matthias Farley, and Zeke Motta headed to the media headquarters for a 45-minute session with the press. Diaco and Te'o sat at the head table in one room, while the other four players all had their own tables in a second room. The Irish contingent enjoyed a police escort, with Lewis-Moore controlling the siren in the lead vehicle.

Practice moved earlier than slated, with the five-bus caravan leaving the Westin Diplomat at 11:20 AM for the Miami Dolphins' practice facility. The ESPN broadcast crew, fresh from doing the Rose Bowl Tuesday, came to practice and visited with Kelly and several assistants and players. After a brisk 75-minute workout under sunny, 80-degree conditions, the Irish squad had lunch in the Dolphins' cafeteria. The

Notre Dame players hydrated extensively in the humid conditions, with most carrying huge jugs of Gatorade away from practice.

Thursday night activities included one dinner for the players—and a separate dinner for the coaching staff.

Friday, January 4

The day began early for Irish offensive coordinator Chuck Martin and five Irish players (Everett Golson, Zack Martin, Tyler Eifert, Theo Riddick, and TJ Jones) as they left the Westin Diplomat at 7:30 AM for their press conference at the media hotel in Ft. Lauderdale. Chuck Martin and Golson took center stage in one room, while the other four players spoke at individual tables in a second room. Coach Martin spoke about how the Irish have talked about being the last team to turn in its equipment for the year—and that goal will be accomplished by playing in the BCS title game on Monday. He also noted that as the former head coach and assistant at Grand Valley State, this marks the seventh time in 12 years he has finished the year playing for a national championship (he won four of those at Grand Valley State—two as an assistant and two as head coach). Said Martin, "That's more fun than you should be allowed to have."

Next it was off to the Dolphins' practice facility about 10:30 AM for a second day of work at the Miami NFL complex. Among visitors at practice were former Irish quarterback Brady Quinn (now with the Kansas City Chiefs) as well as current Dolphins tight end (and former Irish star) Anthony Fasano. Current Dolphins head coach Joe Philbin spoke to the team briefly before practice.

After another workout in 84-degree conditions, the Irish returned to their hotel for an afternoon at the beach for the coaches and staff and their families, followed by a barbecue beach bash for the team.

Next up on Saturday is media day for both full teams at Sun Life Stadium—the hour-long Irish portion begins at 11:00 AM.

Saturday, January 5

The Irish squad jumped on their buses at 10:30 AM to head to Sun Life Stadium for an hour-long media day session—in partly sunny, warm, humid, and breezy conditions. The Super Bowl–like setup featured separate platforms for Brian Kelly, Manti Te'o, Zack Martin, Everett Golson, Kapron Lewis-Moore, and Tyler Eifert.

Notre Dame's team returned to the hotel for lunch, then left again at 3:30 PM for its workout at the Miami Dolphins' complex. Immediately after practice, Kelly headed to the media hotel in Ft. Lauderdale to receive the Eddie Robinson Coach of the Year Award at a reception sponsored by the Fiesta Bowl and the Football Writers Association of America. Eddie Robinson Jr. was part of the presentation—and former Irish star Derrick Mayes served as master of ceremonies. Kelly then headed to Miami Beach for a private dinner with his coaching staff. The Irish team had dinner in the hotel followed by a comedy show.

Meanwhile the pep rally on South Beach featured remarks from master of ceremonies Mike Golic, Lou Holtz, Joe Theismann, Tony Rice, Pat Terrell, and Martin Short—with an estimated 20,000 fans in attendance.

Sunday, January 6

Coach Brian Kelly left the Westin Diplomat with a delegation of Irish athletics officials at 8:00 AM Sunday to go to the Ft. Lauderdale media hotel for the final press conference of the week. Kelly and Alabama coach Nick Saban posed separately and together with the BCS Coaches'

Trophy, with hordes of photographers recording the moment. Then Kelly spent a half-hour answering questions in front of a packed ballroom. From there, a group of Notre Dame officials headed to Sun Life Stadium for the 10:00 AM NCAA Pregame Bowl Meeting that lasted 30 minutes and detailed all the events of game day.

The Irish players enjoyed some free time in the middle of the day, then returned for a 3:00 PM team Mass, followed by a team meeting and then position meetings. At 4:40 PM the Notre Dame team departed for Sun Life Stadium to take a team photo in blue game jerseys and do a brief walk-through on the pristine green field.

A group of Notre Dame athletics administrators attended the evening BCS National Championship Gala at the Miami Seaquarium—with most of the college football world in attendance.

Monday, January 7

Here's what the Irish are up to on game day:

9:30 AM	Breakfast
10:45 AM	45-minute final shake-out/walk-through
Noon	Lunch
12:30 PM	Offensive and defensive meetings
5:00 PM	Pregame meal
5:35 PM	Leave for Sun Life Stadium
6:05 PM	Arrive Sun Life Stadium

ESPN requested three quick interviews with Brian Kelly at Sun Life Stadium—one when the team arrives, a second as the teams take the field for warm-ups, and a third just prior to kickoff.

A Pac-12 Conference crew will officiate the game tonight.

Just hours before tonight's final matchup of the college football season, Liberty Mutual Insurance, in partnership with the National Football Foundation and the College Football Hall of Fame, celebrated the impact coaches have on their players, school, and community by announcing the 2012 Liberty Mutual Coach of the Year Award winners. The annual award—which honors sportsmanship, integrity, responsibility, and excellence on and off the field—recognizes one coach in each NCAA division, and the 2012 winners included Brian Kelly of Notre Dame in the Football Bowl Subdivision. Each 2012 Coach of the Year Award winner receives a $50,000 donation from Liberty Mutual Insurance to the charities of his choice, as well as a $20,000 scholarship grant in his name to his school's alumni association. The winners were chosen through fan voting cast December 4 to 20 and by selection committees comprised of national media and College Football Hall of Fame players and coaches. Fan votes contributed 20 percent to each coach's final score, while media and College Football Hall of Famers' ballots accounted for 25 percent and 55 percent, respectively.

A devoted supporter of charity and education, Kelly's on-field success is matched by his community work off the field. In 2008 Kelly and his wife, Paqui, started the Kelly Cares Foundation, which has an emphasis on breast cancer research, education, and awareness. The Kellys also provided a $250,000 gift to the University to support cancer research, Notre Dame's Hesburgh Library system, and the Robinson Community Learning Center, which provides tutoring, violence-prevention programs, youth entrepreneurship, and performing arts projects for at-risk families in South Bend. Kelly also has established a $250,000 endowment scholarship for football players at his alma mater, Assumption College. Kelly's student-athletes also thrive in the classroom, with an academic progress rate score that is nearly 20 points higher than the FBS average. This year, four Irish players were named to the Hampshire Honor Society, earned by achieving a minimum 3.2 grade-point average throughout their college careers; two players were named first-team Academic All-Americans; and, for the second consecutive year, the program produced a National Football Foundation National Scholar-Athlete.

With the BCS title game later that evening, Kelly was unable to attend the presentations at a Ft. Lauderdale hotel. Finally, after five weeks of buildup and hype, kickoff at Sun Life Stadium arrived for Notre Dame and Alabama, after a busy day of tailgating for fans:

Unbeaten and top-rated Notre Dame's first crack at a Bowl Championship Series title game didn't exactly end the way the Irish hoped. But credit second-ranked and once-beaten Alabama, a veteran at these kinds of games, for making all the right moves in a 42–14 victory at Sun Life Stadium that handed the Tide its third BCS crown in four seasons.

It started on a tough note for the Irish (12–1), as Alabama (13–1) roared out of the gate to a 28–0 halftime lead after scoring on its first three possessions and rolling up 202 yards in the first period alone.

Notre Dame, meanwhile, struggled early on both sides of the ball. By halftime the Irish had already given up more points than they had in any game this season, the previous high being 26 in a triple-overtime win over Pittsburgh. The most yards Notre Dame gave up this season was 379; Alabama cracked the 500 mark early in the fourth quarter.

Alabama looked the part of a BCS champion—while the Irish walked away understanding what it takes to make it this far and maybe appreciating what the Tide was able to do to carry off the final chapter.

Notre Dame arrived at the title game on the cusp of what would have been a fantasy scenario, that of being unranked at the start of the season and the undisputed champions at the end of the campaign. However, a dominating ground game and timely passing by Alabama quarterback AJ McCarron made the Tide offense seemingly impossible to stop in the opening two periods.

Eddie Lacy ran for 140 yards on 20 attempts (one TD), and T.J. Yeldon added another 108 yards and a score of his own on 21 attempts. McCarron always seemed to make the right plays in the passing game, connecting on 20 of his 28 throws for 264 yards and four TDs.

The Irish had hoped to establish at least some sort of ground game against the top-rated Tide defense—but that proved to be almost

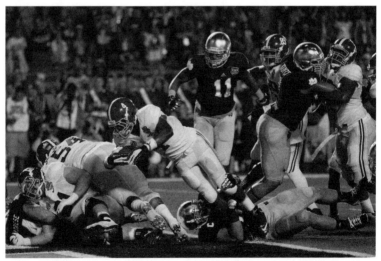

Alabama's T.J. Yeldon dives in for a touchdown during the BCS title game in Miami. In their 42–14 win over Notre Dame, the Crimson Tide were able to run the ball against the Irish, something no other team was able to do all season long. Photo courtesy of AP Images

impossible. The Irish managed only 32 net rushing yards (37 on 10 carries by Theo Riddick), as they were forced to throw the football as the Tide built its advantage.

Notre Dame's Everett Golson threw for 270 yards and a score (a six-yard TD to Riddick), but his 21-for-36 effort came as the Irish played from the back all night long. TJ Jones had a career-high seven receptions (90 yards), and DaVaris Daniels contributed six grabs for a career-best 115 yards—while tight end Tyler Eifert had six for 61 yards.

Senior safety Zeke Motta led both teams with 16 tackles, and all-star senior linebacker Manti Te'o had 10. But Alabama simply proved hard to stop in rolling up a 529–302 advantage in total yards—including a 265–32 advantage on the ground. The Irish weren't helped by losing senior defensive captain Kapron Lewis-Moore to a first-half knee injury—with nose guard Louis Nix III limping much of the second half.

The Irish had only a single turnover (an interception by Alabama on the opening series of the second half). But Notre Dame's defense uncharacteristically could not get off the field, yielding TD drives of 82, 61, 80, 71, 97, and 86 yards—as Alabama finished with a 38:13 to 21:47 advantage in time of possession.

Obviously, the game went just opposite of everything we wanted to do defensively and offensively. It really needed to be close for us to stick to our game plan. We get behind and we've got to sling it around, trying to play catchup, which Everett [Golson] did a pretty good job of making a difference in the offensive game. I felt like he was getting better and better as the game went on. It was disappointing that it was one of those days. Were they more ready to go? I think they were more ready for that moment. I don't think our preparations were an issue, our kids had good practices. It's 21–0 in the first quarter, and you're kind of fighting an uphill battle. It is what it is. We could have used that fumble on the punt, and then maybe we punch it in and it's 7–7. But we needed some good things to happen early to get it going, and it didn't happen. Credit to them because they didn't allow us to have early success.

—Chuck Martin

Notre Dame was the first team in the Bowl Championship era to play for the national title after starting a season unranked. The Irish already were the first team to climb from unranked to the nation's top spot since Missouri in 2007. Since opening the 2011 season with an 0–2 record, Notre Dame has won 20 of its last 24 games—good for an .833 winning percentage. The Irish have the seventh-best overall FBS and fifth-best BCS AQ winning percentage since September 17, 2011.

Notre Dame blanked nine of its 12 football opponents in the first quarter during the regular season, but Alabama became the first Irish foe to collect a touchdown in the opening 15 minutes. Miami, Oklahoma, and Pittsburgh were the other teams to score against the Irish in the opening 15 minutes (all field goals). The Irish had not previously surrendered a touchdown in the first quarter since November 26, 2011, against Stanford—a span that extended over 14 games.

Alabama scored 14 points in the first quarter tonight, which exceeded the total of Notre Dame foes over the entire regular season. The Irish had allowed just nine points in the first quarter over their 12 regular season games. Notre Dame had outscored its opponents in the regular season by an 85–9 margin in the first quarter. Notre Dame had outscored its past two opponents (Wake Forest and USC) by a combined 31–0 in the opening quarter.

With Notre Dame having secured a winning record this season, Brian Kelly is the first Irish coach to register a winning record over three straight seasons since Lou Holtz in 1994–1996, and the first Notre

Dame coach to register three consecutive winning seasons to open his Irish coaching career since Dan Devine in 1975–1977.

Sophomore quarterback Everett Golson started 11 games in 2012 and led the Irish to victories in 10 of those football contests. The 10 straight wins (in 10 starts) to open a career was the second-most in school history. Bob Williams holds the school record as he guided Notre Dame to victories in his first 11 career starts. Golson is the first quarterback in school history to lead the Irish to road victories over top 10 foes in his first two respective road starts. Golson threw for at least 200 yards in six different games this season, including each of the last five outings.

The six rushing touchdowns this season for Golson are the most for an Irish signal-caller since Jarious Jackson had seven in 1999. Golson is the first Irish quarterback with a rushing touchdown in a bowl game since Kevin McDougal in the 1994 Cotton Bowl. Golson has recorded both a rushing touchdown and passing touchdown in the same game on five different occasions this season (Purdue, Michigan State, Pittsburgh, Boston College, and Alabama).

Senior tight end Tyler Eifert—the 2012 Mackey Award recipient and 2011 finalist—turned in another solid performance in his final college game, tying his season high with six catches for 61 yards against Alabama. Eifert's six catches also matched his best production in a bowl game, duplicating his six receptions (for 90 yards) in the 2011 Champs Sports Bowl. Thirty-four of Eifert's 50 catches this season resulted in a touchdown or first down. Eifert led the Irish this season with 12 receptions of at least 20 yards. Of his 140 career catches, 30 went for at least 20 yards. Eifert ranks No. 1 in school history in both career receptions (134) and career receiving yards (1,779) by a tight end. Eifert's 50 catches and 685 receiving yards this season both rank third among tight ends in school history, with Eifert now holding two of the top three spots on both lists.

Senior linebacker Manti Te'o led the Irish with 113 tackles in 2012. He also led Notre Dame with 128 stops, $13^1/_2$ tackles for loss, and five sacks in 2011. Te'o collected 100 or more stops in each of the last three seasons, becoming the second player in school history and first since Bob Crable (1979–1981) to surpass 100 tackles in three straight seasons.

Sophomore wide receiver DaVaris Daniels collected his first career 100-yard receiving game, registering six catches for a game-high 115 yards against Alabama. His previous career high for receiving yards was 86 against Pittsburgh on November 3. Daniels' 115 yards were the most by an Irish receiver this season, and most since October 29, 2011, when Michael Floyd tallied 121 yards on six catches in a 56–14 win over Navy at Notre Dame Stadium. Daniels' 115 yards were the most by an Irish receiver in a bowl game since the 2008 Hawaii Bowl, when Golden Tate piled up 177 yards on six catches in a 49–21 win over Hawaii.

Senior safety Zeke Motta finished with a career-best 16 tackles against Alabama, the most by an Irish player this season and the most since September 25, 2010, when Manti Te'o had 21 tackles against Stanford. Motta's nine assisted tackles tied a Notre Dame bowl record first set by Jay Case at the 1979 Cotton Bowl against Houston.

We made great strides in three years. But we also know that we've climbed a lot of rungs of the ladder, but we haven't gotten to the top of the ladder yet. But that's life.

What did we learn? We learned that, hey, we've come a long way in three years, and we're certainly going to take pride in the 2012 season because it's an incredibly awesome season for tons of different reasons.

We had won the battle of the trenches for 12 games. But not against Alabama. So there is another level of power football that is still out there—we have to and will continue to close that gap. We got pretty close, and that was great. Now let's go back to working as opposed to trying to overanalyze. We're pretty good at not overanalyzing. We're good at watching the tape and being realistic with what we did well and didn't do well.

But Coach Kelly is always asking us and we're asking each other, what did we do well today? What are our shortcomings? And his ability to admit the shortcomings is one of his biggest strengths, in my opinion. If your kids want to buy in and we're short in an area, let's work hard in that area to get better. But if we're not good at it, let's find another way to win. And all of the things that go into winning and getting the kids to be realistic, that's a fine line. How do you get their confidence up and still convince them there's work to do because maybe we are not good enough yet? Trust in what Coach Kelly does—figuring out what gives his team the best chance to win.

—*Chuck Martin*

I have no problem with the plan. We just didn't have the manpower necessary to do the things that we would have liked to have done. With six offensive linemen that could actually practice, you're going to lose out on a lot of things that you would like to do. We needed to play Alabama the following week after USC, and that would have been the best situation for us.

What stands out to me was that when we took our team down there, they knew it wasn't a bowl game. The need to worry about curfews, that wasn't there. There was definitely a different sense when you're playing for a national championship than when you're playing in another bowl game. So what stood out to me was the kids' demeanor was very business-like when they went down there. This was another electric environment in the stadium—and that was a hallmark of the 2012 season. Our players relished those moments on the grand stage.

—*Brian Kelly*

Epilogue

The day after Notre Dame's loss to Alabama, the Irish players traveled on their own to their homes, with another week remaining before classes resumed back on campus.

The Notre Dame traveling party, mostly administrators and families, rode their midday charter flight back to South Bend.

Brian Kelly flew to Nashville, where later that night he received the FBS National Coach of the Year Award from the American Football Coaches Association at that organization's annual convention. Kelly qualified as the consensus national coach of the year for 2012.

On February 6, Kelly and his staff watched as 24 new names joined the Irish roster on national signing day—including *USA Today* All-Americans Jaylon Smith, Greg Bryant, and Max Redfield.

On March 20, the Irish began spring drills.

During the 2013 NFL Draft from April 25 to 27, the transition to 2013 became even more official, as Tyler Eifert (first round to Cincinnati), Manti Te'o (second to San Diego), Jamoris Slaughter (sixth to Cleveland), Theo Riddick (sixth to Detroit), Kapron Lewis-Moore (sixth to Baltimore), and Zeke Motta (seventh to Atlanta) all were drafted by NFL teams—while Braxston Cave (Cleveland), Mike Golic Jr. (Pittsburgh), Cierre Wood (Houston), and John Goodman (Cincinnati) all signed free-agent contracts.

And, with faith restored that Notre Dame's football had injected itself into the national conversation for the foreseeable future, the chase for a championship began all over again.

Credits

Thanks to Irish head coach Brian Kelly, assistant head coach and defensive coordinator Bob Diaco, and offensive coordinator Chuck Martin for their insights into the 2012 season.

Thanks to Karen Croake for her proofreading expertise.

Thanks to Brian Hardin and Michael Bertsch for their research into Notre Dame football facts and figures.

Thanks to Michael Bennett and Lighthouse Imaging for their assistance with photographs of the 2012 season.